Crystal Guardians Of Gaia And New Earth

Multidimensional Crystal and Planetary Wisdom

Karen Lithika

This Book is Copyright © 2021 The Crystal Guardians of Gaia and the New Earth: Karen Lithika (the 'Author'). All rights reserved worldwide.

Authors Website: KarenLithika.com

Social Media: Karen Lithika

Reproduction or translation of any part of this work without permission of the copyright owner is unlawful. Requests for permission or further information should be addressed to the Author. No part of this eBook or Paper Book may be translated or reproduced or transmitted in any form or by any means, electronic or mechanical, including photocopying, recording, or by an information storage and retrieval system without the prior written permission of the Author.

The publication is designed to provide accurate and Authoritative information in regard to the subject matter covered, based on the Author's experience and understandings. The Author and publisher do not recommend anything contrary to common sense. If professional medical or nutritional advice or other expert assistance is required, the services of a competent professional person should be sought.

First Published as electronic book in Australia 2022

Published by Harmony Unity Love Publishing™

National Library of Australia Cataloguing-in-Publication entry

Lithika, Karen, author

Crystal Guardians of Gaia and New Earth / Lithika Karen

ISBN: 978-0-6451642-0-6 (electronic version)

ISBN: 978-0-6451642-1-3 (paperback version)

Harmony Unity Love Publishing;

Includes bibliographical references:

Crystal Healing

Acknowledgements

Thank-you Mother, Mother Gaia, Earth, our Goddess

For she is our Mother of Light

To Every Being who acknowledges the Light Journey, the Mission

To heal our World and assist Humanity in reaching a State of Higher Consciousness

To my Light Family, your love and insights along the way

To the Crystals of our World

Thank you for your guidance and light, for your assistance

Love to my Multidimensional Light Family

For you, the reader, feeling the Innate Calling to read these pages

May they serve you in Higher Light Advancement and Wisdom

Infinite Blessings

Welcome

The crystals welcome you, to discover and expand your consciousness, to learn about your spiritual gifts. To connect more deeply to our crystal friends is a life given opportunity, for we are all interconnected as a family of light. I ask you to read this book with an open heart, an open mind full of love and enlightenment, for you will receive this tenfold.

As a Crystal Vibrational Healer, I bring forth this information largely from channelled multi-dimensional beings, including those that represent the Crystal, Plant and Galactic Kingdoms.

I ask you to expand your auric field and connect to every written word which is encoded with a high vibrational light frequency; to raise your consciousness and expand your auric field to a greater level of awareness and understanding.

Know the Crystal Kingdom is assisting the expansion and awakening of our reality. For they are a Legion of Light Beings enhancing and recalibrating the crystalline grid system of Gaia, for they are an integral part of the Biodiversity Matrix.

We ask you to follow your heart guidance and use this information for your own personal journey of light expansion.

May this book provide the guidance you seek and lead you on a path of knowledge and higher light awareness.

Wishing you an abundant and joyful journey.

LOVE=UNITY

Karen Lithika

Table of Contents

A Message to your Light Body — 1

Evolution of Gaia and the Crystal Kingdom — 4

- Wisdom from the Guardians of Gaia — 5
- The Evolution of Gaia and the Biodiversity Matrix — 7
- Crystal and Plant Kingdom — 9
- History and Role of Crystals — 10
- Crystalline Light Matrix of a Crystal — 13
- Crystalline Frequency of a Crystal — 14
- Lemurian Council of Light — 15

Crystal Elemental Beings — 18

- The Elemental Kingdom - Devic Beings — 19
- Plant, Fungi, Animal Devic Beings — 23
- THE ELEMENTALS — 25
- Crystal Devic Beings — 26
- Gabriella the Crystal Deva: A Light Message — 28
- My personal story: The Crystal Deva — 29

The Crystal Guardians — 32

- A Message from the Crystal Collective of Light — 33
- Crystal Akashic Records — 36
- Multi-Dimensional Crystals — 38
- Inner Earth – The Crystal Kingdom — 40

Planetary Ascension and the New Earth — 44

- Planetary Ascension and Beyond — 45
- The New Earth — 47
- Multidimensional Traits of a Lightworker — 50
- New Earth Light Message — 53

CRYSTALLINE LIGHT MESSAGES THE CRYSTAL KINGDOM — 66

- Crystals for Ascension — 67
- Clear Quartz — 69
- Rose Quartz — 75
- Amethyst — 78
- Citrine — 80
- Smoky Quartz — 82
- Selenite — 85
- Moldavite — 88
- Apophyllite — 91
- Herkimer — 93
- Lemurian Quartz — 95

CRYSTAL ATTUNEMENT AND CONNECTION — 98

- Connect to the Crystalline Frequency of a Crystal — 99
- Heart Centred Crystalline Consciousness — 101
- How to Create a personal Crystal connection — 102
- Tools to Assist Your Light Expansion — 103
- Crystal Light Guardian — 107

HIGHER DIMENSIONAL CRYSTAL HEALING — 112

- How Crystals Assist Your Auric Field — 113
- Light Body, Chakras, Crystals — 115
- New Earth Body Template — 116
- Colour Therapy and Crystals — 119
- Crystalline Colour Healing — 120

PERSONAL CARE FOR LIGHT WORKERS — 124

- Awaken to You — 125
- Protecting your Auric Field — 128
- Daily Auric Protection — 130
- A Message from the Sun — 132
- The SUN and DNA ACTIVATION — 133

Ascension & Self Care	134
Create Your Crystal Light Family	136
Creating a Heart Centred Home	139
Crystals for Cleansing and grounding	141
Crystals for Grounding	142
Creative Visualisation with Crystals	144
Cleansing your Crystals	145
Understanding Entities & Attachment	146

CRYSTAL TOOLS FOR EXPANSION AND HEALING — 148

Spiral Dream Weaving	149
The Crystal Grid	151
The Crystal Wand	158
The Pendulum	160

INTRODUCTION

A Message to your Light Body

You are a magnificent being dear one, an infinite being of light brought forth in this timeline to assist your soul development and the great transition of Gaia. Amongst our daily lives, remember who you, a beautiful radiant being of light living in this multidimensional reality.

Your role is to be who you are, just to be, for this is the greatest step in reaching a state of higher awareness and expansion. For we are all on this journey together in a frequency of love. For we share a love of Gaia and for all living beings, for we are one family of universal light working together in unity consciousness. Spend a moment integrating these messages, for this is a key to unlocking greater perception and awareness of who you truly are.

We ask you to work together dear friends, working together in a harmonic convergence of light to assist your own evolvement and alignment. We ask you to remain in close alignment to your heart for this is the key to a fulfilling life. Work together in groups to raise the consciousness of human awareness, focussed on love for rapid awakening and enlightenment. For this is a powerful tool that is easily accessible and infinitely powerful beyond your imagination.

Know the awakening is occurring as many are connecting to a wide audience of like- minded souls and attuning to their inner truth of who they truly are. With this in mind, we ask you to remember the power within dear one, and the infinite goals of your soul journey, for the awakening has commenced. And all inhabitants on earth are assisting in this transmutation, as our crystalline light bodies awaken.

For you see, the crystals are an integral part of Gaia and play a fundamental role in recalibrating her light body to a higher dimensional plane, in this three-dimensional reality. Know your world is now reaching higher dimensional light, light awareness expanding in your world. This assistance also extends to every living being, for the crystals are an integral part in raising your awareness, your multidimensional understanding, enhancing your crystalline light body.

For every crystal is a living being of light, ready to assist your soul journey, by healing and expanding your consciousness in every breath you take, every moment of your reality.

Amongst our current reality, finding the space to read, awaken your consciousness and understanding is fundamental. It will enable you to connect with aspects of yourself that you are not aware of. And with this guidance and assistance by the Crystal Kingdom, a subtle transformation will occur, as you connect more deeply to your own internal awareness and awaken your *crystalline DNA*, resulting in a recalibration of your knowing and understanding of who you truly are.

Follow your flow, take care of your auric field. For the path of the seeker and light worker relates to your own soul journey of acceptance, healing and transformation.

Believe in the magic of your reality and awaken to the higher dimensional light planes, for the crystals will greatly enhance the unfoldment of your reality.

Sending love on your Crystal journey.

Karen Lithika

Evolution of Gaia and the Crystal Kingdom

In this time of transmutation, our beautiful Mother Gaia is evolving. As she evolves, the crystals are assisting every being in reaching a state of Higher Consciousness.

We are more in tune and more attracted to crystals, as our intuition leads us to Crystalline Healing.

Wisdom from the Guardians of Gaia

We are a collective of beings that reside in a higher plane of existence, in an interdimensional space in the upper 4th, all the way to the ninth and beyond. For we integrate and migrate through these dimensions. We come through now as portal openers, to assist in bringing forth the higher vibrational messages to humanity. For we seed many planets with higher dimensional frequencies that are called through like a multidimensional dance to reach humanity in this moment.

For beautiful Gaia is accelerating in her energetic field, her expansion is radiating, and we are all here to assist every being that resides on her surface and within inner earth. We all have a role to play, in this moment of ascension, in the unfolding and expansion of this dimensional space.

Shall we explain the shift that is fast approaching? Yes, I think this will be important for the reader. The expansion was recognised many millennia ago, it was called forth from then to now. For destiny awaits every being, even the planets, for they are living systems, interdimensional beings that resonate such beauty. Like the great whales that swim in your oceans, such awe for their size and mysteries. Our planets have the same mystique for they all resonate their own frequency and vibrational field that allows them to evolve and resonate. Just like every being that resonates and emanates their unique crystalline frequency, which reflects their journey, their mood, their moment and evolvement in this timeline.

Know the planetary upgrade resonates through every being, every tree, crystal, seedling, caterpillar, lion and of course humanity. It is said and we confirm, that every being has a role to play, for every being is part of the Biodiversity Matrix. For we and many assisted in the seeding of Gaia many millennia ago, and we and many beings provided the genetic variation you see on Gaia today, for Gaia is a biodiverse lab, a mixture of gene pools sourced from many planets and universes. And you see, this gene pool is the creation of many civilisations that reside throughout the galaxy. For the creators of Star Wars had much information to pass on.

As the planet was inhabited with a vast array of beings, so too was many other planets. Yet Gaia is a unique planet located in its own constellation, hidden away from many other planets with unique diversity of its own. And the story of Gaia is a beautiful story of time, divergence and a complex history that led Gaia on different paths - that leads us to this moment. This moment of creation for all to see and observe. The universe is responding to this ascension for it is the gateway to many other changes across different timelines and dimensions, as Gaia changes and expands, so too does many other systems. And this is of great importance because it affects civilisation across the universe in many dimensions. For we are all interconnected dear friends, like an ecosystem on your planet, we are all interconnected energetically like a grid work of energetic frequencies all in harmony and sync, and therefore the changes are a symphonic realignment of the energetic fields, which are ultimately transponded throughout the universe. The ascension process is of great energetic change that is subtle and is occurring in every moment. For you see dear friends in this moment, it's like a ripple effect of energetic frequencies. So, the subtle thoughts you speak, the radiance in your words, in your smile are all part of the intergalactic web of energetic frequencies that assist in the ascension process and the unfoldment of the consciousness of Gaia to a higher level.

So, where does this lead us dear friends, to the light and love of all beings, of humanity and the Biodiversity of Gaia. For every inhabitant is derived from love. Love is the universal language of light and throughout the universe to the dimensional gateways of our reality. For love is creation, love is ascension, love is happiness and radiates the highest possible frequencies of peace and harmony. For this is all we seek dear friends, an expanding humanity to reach a higher vibrational level of consciousness.

For the crystals are here to assist our LIGHT Destiny

The Evolution of Gaia and the Biodiversity Matrix

Inception occurred many eons ago, a great meeting took place with a collective of higher dimensional beings for the birthing of Gaia. She began as a crystalline light body in a higher dimensional plane and the collective birthed her physical form which you live on. Her crystalline light body included her story from the point of inception to the three-dimensional matrix and therefore to the development of earth, the physical form. This creation involved a collective of highly evolved beings who developed her crystalline matrices. These matrices are also part of the life force of all beings on this planet, for it comes from the library of light, which is stored in a higher dimensional plane.

Like DNA in this dimension, crystalline DNA can be described as a crystalline rainbow encoded DNA structure for the purposes of your understanding. It holds the crystalline structure of each being that is inhabited on Earth which is also integrated in the crystalline matrix grid of Gaia. As part of creating her crystalline light body, it also included the grid lines and ley lines that are incorporated throughout the planet, which interconnects to her crystalline light body.

The Biodiversity Matrix and Unity Consciousness

The function of nature

As Gaia was created, initiated, a great selection of beings throughout the Galaxy were assigned to be part of this role. This being said, their crystalline DNA was brought forth and reassimilated to be incorporated into the Crystalline Grid of Gaia, developed in its unique grid known as the *Biodiversity Matrix*. Layers apon layers of timelines were initiated, developed in light, providing the multidimensional framework of light.

Amongst the creation of many beings, the ecological framework was also developed, which is recognised as a field in science know as Ecology. This relates to how species co-occur in a harmonic energetic pattern, which enables all beings to live in harmony in this reality. This pattern occurs in every living biological system, in our oceans and on the dry land. As species have evolved together in a diversity of environments, from the deserts to wet rainforests. Each individual holds their unique crystalline matrix of light, their unique relationships with other beings, co-occurring together in a unique form of unity consciousness.

As all beings have agreed to this system, this is the beautiful frequency you feel when you enter a uniquely evolved natural system. It is derived from a millennium ago, a natural crystalline framework of biodiversity, showcasing the myriad of genetic diversity on Gaia, working in sync and in a harmonic divergence of light, known as the *Biodiversity Matrix*. It is the language of the universe harmony and light.

The *Biodiversity matrix* is a Crystalline Grid layer which is incorporated into the main framework of Gaia and serves as the story of nature. The cosmic connection of creation and the beings that we know and love, have a great galactic history. For their genetic origins are sourced far and wide throughout the galaxy. And this is the story of creation.

Each time period in evolution is a crystalline matrix layer that was created in a higher dimensional plane and incorporated into the crystalline matrix of Gaia. This is the story of Gaia from her infancy eons ago, to reach this point in her timeline. For in the higher dimensional planes, magic occurs at levels we are unaware of.

Gaia became integrated into a crystalline grid system of light, composed of numerous matrixes encoded with a wealth of information, which is the story of biodiversity on this planet. However, her story line was interrupted resulting in changes to her story/timeline as a result of the agenda of others. This also relates to the moment we have reached in our timeline, cumulative effects that have resulted in our current reality.

The great planetary shift, the planetary alignment of Saturn and Jupiter, December 2020. The planetary light assimilation resulting in the initiation of the New Light Age. The beginning of a new light trajectory, a new timeline for our construct. Infinite beams of love and higher light consciousness now shower our world, as we move towards a reality of higher consciousness.

Crystal and Plant Kingdom

The collective light bodies of the Crystal and Plant Kingdom occur above and below ground level. Their role is two-fold in the third dimension and beyond.

Both the Crystal and Plant Kingdoms are an integral part of the crystalline grid structure of Gaia which is a layer of her crystalline grid system. This grid system works in recalibrating her energetic field and functioning at a high energetic level. For they are part of her crystalline grid system in this dimension and other dimensions.

This grid structure is rarely seen in the third-dimensional reality but can be observed in a space of enlightened awareness. They form part of the crystalline make up of Gaia and were integrated at her birthing. For this is a long story of creation, that began eons ago. Amongst their roles, the plant and crystal kingdoms both assist all living beings, as the recorded history tells the story of the many benefits of crystals and plants used by humanity and all beings.

History and Role of Crystals

Crystals hold a telecommunication function at a deep interdimensional level, linking aspects of Gaia to the Crystalline Universe and are part of her Crystalline Grid Structure. They serve the role as teleportal openers and vibrational enhancers for all beings.

Crystals were first encoded into the crystalline matrix of Gaia at the inception of her planetary light body. As Gaia's crystalline light body was encoded with the unique crystal matrices, they were then created into a solid formation to align with our three-dimensional timeline. Fundamentally, all of these layers provide a multi-functional role in maintaining the integral structure of the planet, but also function at a higher dimensional level, as messengers/portal openers to assist in the transponder of high vibrational frequencies that are regularly recalibrated in the three-dimensional timeline and beyond.

Crystals contain light encoded information directed from the universe, to upgrade the consciousness of Gaia and every being that resides in her energy field. They are conductors of light, portal openers to other dimensions. They are intricate beings that have multifunctional uses. By creating a specific grid or visiting an ancient site where earlier ancestors have developed their own technologies, this information is still imprinted on Gaia. Ancient technologies can be accessed if you are aligned and imprinted with this knowledge. Such sites can be interconnected to crystal beds located underground or large subsurface clusters. To reach another dimension can occur by journeying through your third eye and your light field. For we are powerful infinite beings, capable or undertaking such wonderful experiences.

In this timeline, to reach this level of awareness and entrance to the higher realms is available to some but will become more accessible to many as the consciousness of Gaia expands in our three-dimensional reality. On a daily basis, light encoded crystalline rays of light are showering Gaia. *Visualise* that for a moment, for all beings are showered by the love of Mother Gaia, the Sun and the Universe. This is assisting the raising of our consciousness to a higher level which is being integrated into our light bodies in every moment.

The Crystal Kingdom is assisting the recalibration of this information, enabling our ascension process to be a smoother process for the collective of beings that reside on Gaia and the transition in the universe.

Amongst the individual crystalline signature of each crystal, know they are encoded with a high frequency of love, of the highest vibrational light. Staying in this vibrational level of awareness, in a heart centred space will greatly assist you in reaching a deeper connection to Gaia and the Crystal Kingdom.

Crystals play a functional role in healing your auric field and connecting to the energetic pulse of every cell in your body. The rhythm and pulse of our energetic field can directly relate to the atmosphere of our surroundings. When you examine this at an energetic level, you come to understand that we all resonate at a certain frequency, all beings do, and so do the crystals. With this information, we are becoming more connected to this aspect of ourselves, intuitively connecting to a finer level of resonance within, as we connect to the subtle vibrational energy that is showering our planet, which resonates and vibrates in every cell of our body, for fundamentally we are made of particles of light which are triggered by light wave particles that resonate in every living cell, every organ, reaching our auric field.

For once you align and become aware of the subtle energy field, you become more integrated into yourself and more aware of every thought that enters your mind, every drop of energy your body emits, your auric field and every living being. This deep connection with yourself is part of the transition that is taking place, for it is the deeper connection that is enabling you to reach different aspects of your auric field and deeper aspects of your higher self. For this is the true awakening, becoming more connected to who you really are, and everything in your environment, every being. And with this awakening, you will become more connected to the energetic fields of every living being, the energy field of every aspect of every part of you.

And with this knowledge, you will accept the greater knowing of life and the complexities of your own vessel, the human body and how this relates to the timeline you are living in, in this very moment. For this is the true essence of your awakening, to reach this level of awareness and reach a higher state of consciousness.

And this is where crystals can assist, for crystals are pure crystalline light beings of universal light that are naturally integrated within our auric field, for we are all made of the same crystalline light language, a universal code, universal building blocks of life.

The crystalline matrices of crystals are designed to work within our auric fields for we are integrated as a family of light, working together in synergistic energetic union. For our crystalline DNA matrices align and work together in harmony. For crystals are designed to raise our vibrational fields, clear disharmony and cleanse our world.

In every moment crystals are healing and radiating a high vibrational frequency. If you think of Rose Quartz, imagine the magnificent frequency of love and harmony that is showering our planet. I ask you now to imagine this, imagine all of the Rose Quartz Crystals throughout the world resonating their frequency. Regulating energetic downloads and enhancing our existence through their energetic resonance of light. It is our time to awaken to our crystal friends, to awaken our understanding to our own crystalline frequency of who we are, so we can become more integrated into our own mission, wisdom and insight. And thus, more connected to our crystalline light alliances.

Crystalline Light Matrix of a Crystal

Crystals are multidimensional beings of light. Each crystal is encoded with the very makeup of its own creation, its crystalline DNA lineage of light. Amongst the physical form we see, within is the seeding of the crystalline light which also emanates throughout the crystal, also known as the auric presence around the crystal. Each type of crystal has its own unique crystalline light signature, a crystalline blueprint encoded with a specific role and healing function.

Crystals are derived from the universe and like us were placed on Gaia with a purpose, vision and mission. Within each crystal can be a devic being, or a devic being can be responsible for a cluster or family of crystals that grow synergestically together. Energetically the devic being is connected to every piece of crystal as their key role is to nurture and facilitate the connection between the physical and crystalline/spiritual aspect of the crystal on planet earth.

A large crystal can be broken up into many pieces but will still contain and emanate the unique crystalline frequency for that particular type of crystal. Some crystals occur in many parts of the planet, a good example is clear quartz, transmitting light encoded information in different areas of the world. Crystals are also encoded with additional light encoded information for that particular region. This can have multiple roles specifically to the balancing and maintaining of Gaia's Crystalline Light body. Our ancient ancestors have also downloaded information in crystals, located in particular region of Gaia.

The crystalline frequency of a crystal is designed and encoded to work with the auric field of any being. For we are all integrated as a family of light. To understand how a crystal can assist you can be discovered by creating a deep connection to yourself first and awakening to your intuition and higher chakras/light body. This will enable you to have a deeper connection with your higher self and naturally become connected to crystal wisdom.

The soul purpose of a crystal is to assist Gaia and all of her inhabitants reach a greater connection and awakening to their light mission. The vast array of different crystals can be seen like a range of different groups of plants in a forest. The unique crystalline signature of a crystal is specifically encoded to assist our life force, evolved on Gaia for a specific crystalline reason. Know these ancient crystalline frequencies are encoded with the life force, crystalline codes of all beings. Specifically, to integrate and align to the crystalline frequency of all life.

Crystalline Frequency of a Crystal

The crystalline frequency of a crystal is a unique energetic crystalline signature of light that constitutes a particular crystal type. It is a unique light encoded high vibrational passage of information within the crystalline DNA of a crystal.

Citrine and Clear Quartz both share the same overarching crystalline structure that makes them part of the Quartz family, this can be seen in physical characteristics relating to the quartz structure, formation and shape. However, if you close your eyes and picture each crystal next to each other, open your third eye to a higher level of vision. You may sense the subtle crystalline differences. Colour is also a good visual indication of the difference between Clear Quartz and Citrine.

Each crystal is composed of a labyrinth of energetic frequencies that relate to their personal intention as a crystal on Gaia; their crystalline purpose. This frequency is part of the underlying crystalline genetic makeup of the crystal. Another way to describe this is our light bodies for they are part of our intergalactic genetic heritage and the same concept can be applied to every living being including crystals.

Lemurian Council of Light

Know we are your ancestors, like many before us, as the metamorphosis of your timeline aligns with our mission of light. See us as a window to your future, for your transformation is an integral part of the construct of your reality.

Our interest in your story, relates to our own journey of mishaps, triumphs and challenges as a species of light, within the universal laws of the galaxy. Know many are awakening to your Lemurian DNA, an aspect of your DNA lineage of light. For this is an important part of your process, part of understanding the story of humanity in this now moment, your Pleiadian, Atlantean connection and the history of your planet. Know we are just one piece of the puzzle dear ones, one piece of your ever-expanding construct. As the pieces join, as the energies continue to unite, as the past meets the present. The story of your reality becomes clearer as the metamorphosis continues.

Like the Atlanteans, we worked closely with the crystalline frequency of crystals aligned with the Pleiadians and many other beings. See us as your distant ancestors for our interest in your species and evolvement is fundamental to our own survival. Know specific crystals in your world hold the technology of our civilisations. You have the opportunities to activate this crystalline frequency. For it is interrelated to your own DNA alignment, your own past life crystalline journey.

We come today to activate and awaken you. To acknowledge the construct you are in and to see the great future that is before you. To see the activation and expansion of you, the amplification and expansion of your role. The knowledge of knowing within, beyond the timeline you exist in, beyond the controlled narrative of your world.

We ask you to seek the crystals, the vibrational connectors of your world, to acknowledge the instrument of light they are and the unlocking of their universal power is apon you. To connect to the crystals and stones of your area, to the crystalline grid, the expansion of your reality. To know they are of great assistance now in your Expansion Transition to Light. To see their own crystalline framework amplifying integrating with your field and assisting your multidimensional expansion.

To understand your role, and to see the role of others who are assigned to specific tasks in your reality. For the layers of light within are awakened more in others and to acknowledge this. To know this relates to stories and lives of long ago, of past activations, of past events leading to this very moment. As torch bearer of the new reality, there are those on your earth that have agreements in providing information of light, upgrading areas of your construct and working with stories from long ago. See us as your allies, as we collectively journey to light.

Crystal Elemental Beings

We welcome you to our Crystalline Light World, where the magic of Higher Light Alliance shines.

A world of Infinite Harmony and Happiness

Infinite Rainbow Colours of Light

The Elemental Kingdom - Devic Beings

A general introduction - *The Golden Light Collective*

The elementals, also known as Devic beings assist the light flow of higher light frequencies for all beings. Their roles are numerous and vast, with many assisting Gaia's energetic grid system in the higher light dimensions. As your consciousness expands, their presence becomes easier to feel in your current dimensional reality. Know, as your realm becomes lighter and brighter, every being is seen in a light embodiment form, in a ray of multiple colours.

Your world is a wonderful creation of life, of great biodiversity and wonder. As the Higher Light Assimilation is now taking place, your connection to the higher realms becomes more transparent day by day, moment by moment.

The devic beings assist all beings, for they follow the universal laws of creation that govern the Light Universe. Know our ancestral journeys are part of creation, in this realm and in the higher realms.

> ***Every devic being is devoted to assisting the crystalline frequency of Gaia.***

Know, devic beings have many roles to play in fostering the energetic pathways of wind, fire, air and water. They are fundamental to the stewardship of Gaia, integrating higher dimensional frequencies and maintaining the natural earthly weather processes we know. A hierarchical group of beings who work in symphony to cleanse, coordinate and replenish the main natural features of Gaia. In saying hierarchical, I refer to an order, a way of determining roles, like a food web. Each elemental assists each other in their role for this is the same system that occurs on earth within our natural ecosystems. They also assist individual beings in their crystalline welfare, assisting with their connection to Mother Gaia and all beings.

Many devic groups specifically assist in managing the crystalline light network that evolved eons ago, which includes a suite of unique crystalline light signatures that we interpret as living beings, referred to as species. This includes animals, plants, fungi and a myriad of other beings (bacteria) that live in the soil and air. This was designed in the early stages of development, at a time when inception began. For the hierarchical role of beings is visible in our dimension and in the higher realms. For there is an order, an assimilation of roles which were designed to work together in a symphony of light, in a way which allows individuals to be presented with particular tasks amongst their many duties that are innate within their vehicle, their cellular body.

Elemental beings also assist many stages of development and growth. They nurture and balance the energetic field of every being. For the human body is nurtured by millions of bacteria. Our auric field is nurtured by angelic beings and our soul team, our guardians and wayshowers including elementals.

Our humanitarian role is two-fold, for we have our unique light journey to attend to, yet amongst this we have an inherent responsibility to take care of our physical vehicle for the goodness of our own journey, and to be the caretakers of life, biodiversity, Mother Earth.

With the unfolding of our new reality, universal light codes are transmutated from higher dimensions into our three-dimensional reality. I see these in my third eye as a showering of light encoded pockets of information showering our planet. We are starting to see light codes – the changing colour of the sun, complexities of light rays, rainbows, clouds, our atmosphere provides clues of the inherent changes that are occurring.

A good example is when sensitive healers discuss the energies, they feel approaching the planet. It is interpreted as the showering of planetary waves of light. Physical symptoms are felt, typically emotional sensitivity, tiredness, headaches, and for some even physical pain. This is all part of the unfolding of our reality, the unfolding of the true awareness of our light bodies and integrating the new crystalline frequencies into our third dimensional reality.

The devic beings ensure this transmutation is delivered successfully and the light downloads occur and integrate in every living being, which is an innate objective of their tasks. For personal integrations, a suite of physical attributes must be aligned relating to incidents occurring in this lifetime or in other lifetimes. Additionally, this could be impacted by soul agreements with other beings from previous lives.

On planet earth, know a wave of energetic healers are transforming the lives of many. I ask you to connect to this concept for a healer can assist in the transformation of your etheric field and myriad healing requirements. For the devic beings are aware of your journey, your soul contract and your physical health. For as you enter a forest, walk in a garden, devic beings are everywhere, busily working to assist the trees and the flowers. Harmoniously supporting the energetic construct of our reality. Know many elementals could be with you, as part of your soul team. Additionally, they can become integrated with the energy field of your home.

Connecting to devic beings is the simple task of opening your heart to love. Becoming in tune with the natural world. Inviting their connection into your life. Simply set the intention to connect to the elemental kingdom. Place flowers and plants in your home, connect to the natural environment.

There are many tasks for the devic beings who are situated around ley lines, energetic points and sacred sites. For they are all interconnected in such sacred spaces, for there is a concentration of light coded information that is delivered to these regions. There are specific devic beings who work with balancing these high encoded earth points, to ensure the high vibrational frequencies are aligned and transmutated, integrated to our timeline. As well as a range of multidimensional light beings who assist such sacred sites.

Many of us feel the calling to visit sacred sites, natural energetic centres, connecting to the vibrational resonance of Gaia. It could also relate to your DNA activation requirements relating to past life work. For it is an opportunity to receive a unique high vibrational upgrade to your crystalline light body. For many, a reconnection to past life memories, of visitations from previous lives, to receive a deeper connection to your soul template, your life mission.

The integration of high vibrational light codes and releasing these codes back to the Universe and crystalline grid of Gaia. Know the Crystal kingdom has an important role in this light function. To see yourself as an ambassador of Gaia's Light grid, assisting in the transmutation of light coded information, to be transmuted by the human vessel – light body.

Devic beings pride themselves in keeping busy. They view our world in a series of wave formations, crystalline rainbow light particles that work together harmoniously. Know they thoroughly enjoy being of service, assisting humanity and all beings. They are playful wonderful beings, full of creativity joy and wonderment.

There are many kinds of light beings; you may call these faeries which could be classified as devic beings. For there is a myriad of beings including the elves and gnomes. It is simply the task of identifying the light being you are working with and connecting to the vibrational light frequency.

Cultural history has recorded a vast array of beings amongst our forests and natural landscapes that enter our physical domain. There are many forms, many species, with unique personality types, unique motivations and relationships to humanity. It is a journey of unfoldment to learn about the many beings that reside in our multidimensional world. For there are tricksters and lovers of light who reside in a space of unconditional love. So, tread lightly, work in a heart space of love and follow the vibrational frequencies you are feeling. For the journey of communicating with beings in the higher realms requires a level of higher light understanding to develop the skill of reading light signatures and to determine the authenticity of beings.

Plant, Fungi, Animal Devic Beings

Each unique species resonates a light signature, a unique light mission. All beings including the plant, animal, fungi and the crystal kingdom provide their unique light mission and contribution.

As the shift in planetary consciousness continues at a rapid rate, all beings assist the grand light plan. The Plant Kingdom's role is to download light encoded information through the light body of the plant, their physical form for example the leaves filter light information into Gaia, through to inner earth, grounding light through to the root system. The Fungi Kingdom also contribute their unique light affiliation, in many cases interconnected to a plant. For these relationships are termed symbiotic, mycorrhizal – plant and fungi interactions, which result in a net positive gain for both organisms.

See the expansion and complexity of these relationships, beyond your current reality. Understand these relationships extend into the higher light realms. For a myriad of devic beings assist a multitude of beings in your reality simultaneously.

It must be noted that different plant species have different light roles in this complex light world, and thus, it can be appreciated that trees hold a wealth of life force and are fundamental in transferring light information from a higher vibrational field into our dimensional plane. Unique plant species, like wonderful unique crystals all have their unique crystalline light code to transmute. Amongst a forest, special trees have special roles, each with their unique light task, individually and collectively as a light community.

Like a complex crystalline light tapestry, we are all inter-connected as ONE. SEE the oxygen we breathe containing a higher level of Light consciousness; a greater light encoded signature filtrated by the Plant Kingdom through the process of photosynthesis, producing oxygen. Thus, the force field around all beings is working harmoniously, flowing to the landscape and community.

See the great light work of the Plant Kingdom, upgrading and translating the higher light codes from the sun rays combined with water and CO^2. The chemical reaction, the Photosynthetic reaction, resulting in the oxygen we breathe. Upgrading the level of light consciousness for every being to breathe. For as our world upgrades, this chemical light process is fundamental to all beings and the upgrading of our world. This is simply and naturally part of their role amongst many duties. Know the Fungi are intertwined, their hyphae growing, merging, combining assisting the light transmission, transmuting light.

For the Animal Kingdom shares a similar light synthesis with the plant, fungi and crystal world. The devic light beings attuned to assist the Animal Kingdom is simply interrelated to the journey of each unique species and their role in the web of light. Aligned to their unique tasks on earth and their light mission.

THE ELEMENTALS

We are the Sprites, the Undines, the Dwellers of Light
A Living Dance in the Higher Realms
See US in the sprigs of new growth
The delicate rain droplets shining on a leaf
Moments of higher light vibrations
The purity of creation, a connection to US
A Doorway to the Higher Realms
Simple, pure light Opportunities

Elemental Exercise

Simply sit in nature
Close your eyes and smile
Connect to your heart and feel love
When it feels right open your eyes
Observe your surroundings, observe the light
Look for a twinkle, a unique leaf
A smile in nature
The Magic of Life

Simply open your Heart to US
You Will Find Us
The Nature Elementals

Crystal Devic Beings

Crystal devic beings are high vibrational crystalline light alliances. A relationship with a crystal devic being is a special opportunity for growth and higher light expansion. An opportunity to learn about their multidimensional community, interrelated to ancient civilizations situated on the physical plane of Gaia and throughout the universe.

Devic beings are aligned to a family cluster of crystals or an individual crystal. For collectively, all devic beings are interconnected in a network of light, aligning the crystalline network of the particular crystal throughout the crystalline grid of Gaia. They also support the crystalline growing conditions of crystals, ensuring the earth frequencies are in accordance with the energetic requirements in our dimension, a suitable growth platform for the crystal(s).

Devic Beings belong to their own unique crystalline light group lineage. Aligned to specific crystals, relating to the crystalline light signature of the crystal, its unique healing abilities, purpose and mission. Know these are ancient beings, assigned as Guardians of Light, the guardian angels of crystals.

Devic beings co-occur within a labyrinth of light within the crystal. This labyrinth can act as a portal to other dimensions and allows the devic being to move through to other dimensional realms whilst working closely with the crystal.

Unique crystalline devic beings are assigned to certain crystal groups to assist in the Ascension of Humanity and all beings. For example, a race of crystal devic beings are particularly aligned to the Quartz family crystals. These beings are directly related to assisting humanity in the unfolding of consciousness. They have a greater capacity to communicate with humans and integrate our soul journey.

Many other crystals also have this capacity, for example Moldavite crystal devic beings are from a different galactic system. Yet their calling to assist humanity is documented by many. Moldavite has a deep and profound effect on the wearer, causing significant and accelerated shifts in those who connect to the crystalline frequency, assisting Humanities Ascension.

Devic beings are also responsible in protecting light information within a crystal. The occlusions within a crystal can provide clues about crystal devic beings. Know that crystals contain portals to other dimensions, gateways to galaxies and planets.

Ancient civilizations have also stored technologies in crystals. As our world becomes more integrated in Higher Light Consciousness. The information within a crystal could become available, accessible for unique light holders who can access and encode this information.

Connecting to a crystal devic being is a very special encounter. I believe they will not show themselves to just anyone, it must be for a particular reason – a particular journey connection – part of your life purpose that leads you to this moment of connecting to the devic being.

When a crystal is unearthed, the crystal is required to integrate with the surface energy and adjust to the surface energy field. This will also require the devic being to come into their own in a different way, as a different set of crystalline frequencies will be incorporated into the crystal as it adjusts to the surface frequencies. So, you see, the devic beings may reside within the crystal, and in some cases the crystal will just contain the crystalline frequency of the crystal which includes its crystalline healing properties. The devic being can return to the crystal at any time it chooses, for technically it is part of its family of light, its guardianship of Mother Gaia.

Gabriella the Crystal Deva: A Light Message

A message from Gabriella

We are all integrated in this matrix of light called Gaia, the mother. In this light calling, know the crystals are here to assist all those who connect and ask for assistance. For like every being on Gaia, we work in harmony to integrate the frequency and consciousness of the changing tide of ascension and to amplify the frequencies of all beings.

Connecting to a crystal is a crystalline skill. The connection first begins subconsciously as our light bodies naturally weave and integrate, as initially we are attracted to energies that will assist our journey as well as yours, for many reasons. And this connection may be felt in your subconsciousness as a yearning, a desire or craving. It is a way your light body will reach out to your subconscious mind and assist you.

Know we are a gate way to your subconscious, for we contain the crystalline frequency of healing and transmutation. Every crystal, stone and mineral offer this gift. Know some crystals have more concentrated crystalline properties to assist humanity, and you may call it programming at the earlier stages of creation, many eons ago to assist humanity at this time. For everything has a reason, an impression, a journey on Gaia. Follow the crystalline light path to reach us.

My personal story: The Crystal Deva

I feel crystals vibrationally – as their crystalline frequencies ripple through my auric field, followed by energy waves through my physical body. I see crystal beings visually in my consciousness, a beautiful light experience.

These special light connections can be felt vibrationally, like an energetic calling felt in your light body. The crystalline consciousness of the crystalline collective vibrating at a very high vibrational rate, reaching your light field. For the devic being of the crystal is aware of your light evolution and intention. Your soul team are aware of this light connection reaching you. Such connections are now occurring throughout the planet and is a major contributor to the ascension process.

So thus, I share my personal light story of connecting to Gabriella, a crystal devic being within a beautiful Brazilian Quartz. She is a guardian of the light portal within the crystal.

After a series of guided meditations and working on my personal self, I felt my auric field expanding and I knew my sense of awareness and connection to the crystal kingdom was expanding at a rate that was new to me. It was a deep awareness that came over me, and it was validated with the appearance of energetic beings who work with the crystalline kingdom on other planets.

Within the crystal, I instantly connected to worlds within worlds, through the twirling of energies in the crystal. From time to time I would sit with the crystal and see if the same connection was still there and to check if I would have the same connection with any other crystal. The same crystal was standing out energetically, and as each day passed, I came to understand how special this crystal was.

I came to understand a deeper energetic connection to the multidimensional ability of a crystal. In this period, aspects of my higher self, my soul team assisted me through this period of greater awareness.

I decided to sit and meditate with my crystal one afternoon. I asked the crystal is it time to connect, would you like to talk to me. And next I heard yes, hello dear one, for I am Gabriella the devic being within this crystal. Her energy was full of love and excitement, it had a childish, playful resonance. She resonates such love and happiness, which is a beautiful connection to have in one's life.

As I write the next words, Gabriella is with me, as she is a great contributor to this book. Many are now awakening to the greater awareness of our expanding consciousness and the telepathic connections to a range of beings. As the consciousness of our planet continues to expand, these relationships will become more evident and accepted. For our multidimensional selves are radiating and expanding, as we evolve with such abilities.

Gabriella is my Crystal Guardian Angel, a very special crystalline friend. How I cherish the light relationship. May you also find a crystal Guardian Angel to assist your light journey.

The Crystal Guardians

Open your heart to Crystalline Awareness

See Us – Wayshowers of Light

The Crystal Kingdom

A Message from the Crystal Collective of Light

Know we are part of your crystalline light family, the forefathers of creation and initiators of Mother Gaia. We reside in another galaxy, another constellation, in a higher dimension. Our world could be described as a world full of crystals. For we are composed of a multitude of different organisms that contain the crystalline frequency/crystalline signature that is part of the crystals you see in your world.

In our reality, we also have crystals that are slow growing structures, a diversity of crystalline beings in our higher dimensional world. Know the structures that you see in your world is like the diversity in our world.

See our higher dimensional light world like a crystalline forest, encompassing all different kinds of unique crystalline light beings that resonate the crystalline signature of crystals in your world.

Know the crystalline grid of Gaia is connected to the crystalline light signature of every crystal. Particular Crystals in your world have different roles to play, just like your lightworkers, all with their unique missions, see these as the *Crystal Guardians*. It is a broad term to define the clusters, unique crystal formations that serve as light bearers to your crystalline community and our crystalline community. They are strategically positioned throughout your world, located in every corner, many deep within the earth.

Some have surfaced as Gaia has evolved over millions of years and these are fundamental light showers, part of your future and light heritage in your timeline. Many are part of the quartz families which are discussed in more detail in this book. For this is a main reason why they are chosen for discussion.

Crystal Guardians could also be described as large boulders, clusters, crystal points or crystal beds located within the subsurface and deep internal surface of Gaia. Ancient light beings residing deep within Gaia. A fragment from any of these powerful crystals will hold the crystalline resonance and encodement of their mission and a higher light knowledge of their heritage.

Crystal Guardians are the custodians of the Crystalline Grid of Gaia and are portal openers, wayshowers of information to be dispersed at certain points throughout the crystalline grid specifically upgrading your timeline. They are scattered throughout the planet and can appear to be very large natural quartz points many metres high to large granite boulders scattered throughout the landscape. They are encoded with specific light encoded information that is activated and turned on at pivotal moments in your dimensional timeline, frequency upgrades, and activations at certain energy centres. For you see, amongst our way of life, the elemental and crystalline worlds are busily managing and optimizing the crystalline matrix of Gaia, for her own evolution and for every living being. Every crystal seeded on Gaia is waiting for the right time to emerge, grow, expand and shine their crystalline frequency. Playing their part in the evolution of Gaia which in turn resonates throughout the Universe.

Ancient Crystals are deep within the centre of Gaia, to the humble crumbs in your soil. For the events that have occurred on your planet have resulted in areas to be significantly impacted, whilst the earthly functions of your planet also result in erosion and the surfacing of boulders, all part of the reconfigurating and balancing the energies on the surface to her deep core.

***Crystals are conduits of light, amplifiers of the higher vibrational light codes. The Keys to Ancient Technology,
the future of your reality.***

Crystals are the Guardians of Gaia, humble light beings who hold the keys to knowledge and awareness. A major presence of your crystalline reality purposely placed to be turned on at different periods. For their role is like a volcano of light, to assist the transitions, unfolding of light.

Your current timeline is a great example of the Ascension process, and how crystals are assisting the amplification of the crystalline grid of Gaia. They were placed in strategic locations to assist the light transition and the same could be said for your physical/light body, your presence in this timeline. To amplify and enhance Gaia's crystalline light body – from below and above into the geological crust. Like all beings we have a light body which is integrated in the crystalline grid of Gaia.

We send love to every light being who is associated to US. To understand the GREAT LIGHT ALLIANCE THAT IS BEFORE YOU... WITH YOU....

IN UNITY ALLIANCE WE WORK TO ASSIST ALL BEINGS IN YOUR CONSTRUCT

TO UNDERSTAND OUR ROLE IS FUNDAMENTAL TO YOUR ASCENSION

WE ARE YOUR LIGHT FAMILY – MESSENGERS OF LIGHT

Crystal Akashic Records

The Golden Ones

As I flew over Uluru, Central Australia, the Summer of 2019, a group of beings connected to my consciousness. I closed my eyes, and I was invited to enter a golden chamber of light. I saw a portal in my mind open. As I walked through the portal, I was showered with a high vibrational light field of golden energy. This enabled me to enter a space of no time – it was the entrance to the Crystal Akashic Records.

I first became aware of the Crystal Akashic records when I was in communication with a Pleiadian wise elder who is an aspect of my Higher Self. I was invited to enter the Crystal Akashic records, a Selenite labyrinth like cave and I am forever grateful and honoured to be invited – thank you. An Ancient place, of Ancient wisdom and lore. I saw large pillars of Selenite in natural formation, approximately 30 metres in height. The light was dim, as I walked through and felt my DNA awakening, activating the memories of many past lives aligned to this now moment. I felt the presence of tall Ancient Beings, and I instantly connected to past lives in the Pleiades constellation.

The Crystal Akashic records is a location in a dimensional plane where the crystalline history, healing properties and wisdom of all crystals is stored. It also contains the history of many dimensional crystalline beings that reside on many planets that do not occur on Gaia. As I entered this realm, I felt an energy wave of high vibrational light encoded patterns visualise in my mind. At that moment if I could verbalise the complexity of what I saw – it was very difficult to explain in our current third dimensional language. Our verbal word has only so many words and could not explain the vibrational information I received. It took a moment to realise how simple our language is and how restricted we are with our vocal language.

I was introduced to a new group of beings, the care takers of the crystalline frequencies that reside in crystals particularly on Gaia. They explained it as follows:

'We are the beings who originated the crystalline devas and crystalline frequency within crystals in your world. It is a hierarchical approach to this application – like the food chain on planet earth. The ecology of the ecosystems also applies to the devic system who protect and nurture the plants from orchids to large trees. It is a complex system that will be shared to you at a later date, for like the ecology of living beings on planet earth, a similar system is present.'

We have provided you with this information for as a light worker and wayshower, your scientific background as a Botanist has trained you in understanding the complex ecology of the plant systems on Gaia. You have learnt much about the way plants co-occur together and a similar story is told for the crystals, for everything follows the same patterns dear one even on different dimensional planes, and this is the information we wish to share with you.

I have not heard before of the Crystal Akashic records. This is a new concept for me and could be for all that live on Gaia. As the consciousness of the crystalline grid raises to a higher vibrational level – our capabilities to reach these places will become easier. Although like the Akashic records, you need a reason to use the records and be at a certain vibrational frequency to connect, travel and access such places. Many of us are now opening to this reality of acceptance and connection.

***May your Light Journey continue to unfold**
In Love and Unity for all Beings*

Karen Lithika

Multi-Dimensional Crystals

A Crystalline Light Message

Family of Light, Crystalline Wayshowers

For we are all living our light path, following the light of the timeline and construct we reside. Understand your world is like mine, with the same basic patterns of life, the same crystalline flow, aligned to the Galactic origin of creation.

My world is infinitie light, portals upon portals of higher light expansion. An infinite spectrum of colours reaching myriad points of higher light creation. For in the higher dimensions we are more integrated in a Harmonic Light Flow with the living creation of source. It is a unified field of light that we glow, enabling us to feel at peace, a higher spectrum of love flows through us, resonating in every crystalline aspect of us. Each thought can manifest creation, a crystalline light flow connected to the construct of life and all that we desire to fulfill our crystalline light wishes.

We only seek a high vibrational existence because we are completely at peace and in flow with the universe. Every being in our world in attuned to this crystalline light concept that flows through each and every one of us. We are nourished with high dimensional light foods, implicated by a process that ensures all beings are aligned to the higher light view of creation. It is simply the way of higher dimensional living, requiring just a high vibrational thought to manifest.

In the Higher Dimensions, you are always in alignment with source. You are immersed in a Higher Light Stream of higher vibrational light capacity.

Like the myriad Biodiversity of your world, Mother Gaia is home to a wealth of beings represented throughout the Universe. She is the caretaker of life of so many beings. Galactic genetic origins resonate in your world. Your planet could be viewed as a platform of life creation. Of infinite light intelligence streaming through your light construct.

Like a forest of Light in your world, see the crystals in fields of great forests in other dimensions. Of crystalline worlds containing a myriad of crystalline light beings that reside in the crystalline light matrix that is a crystal. In a fluid state of physical formation coupled with crystalline light formations enabling a crystal to merge from a physical state of expansion to a fluid crystalline state. In your world, crystals are largely restricted to a physical shape that is constant. However, as your world expands in a higher light awakening, you will find the crystals of your world will merge and change their crystalline frequency and shape in accordance with the changing consciousness of your world. Observe your crystals, as they flow and align to the universal expansion of your construct.

For the ebbs and flows of your world now align with the higher will of the universe.

Know in the Higher Dimensions, the crystals are part of the Kingdom of Light. Their own unique Kingdom, an original light construct, aligned to the module of creation in all dimensions. They are a tool used throughout the Galaxy, throughout the universe. They are infinite in creation and part of many light families throughout the Galaxy, throughout the universe of Light.

Your world holds the basic instructions of the Crystal world, for you to see and grasp. As your Crystalline Light language is turned on to a higher vibrational light capacity. Much more information will be shared in the future. As your world is currently in a space of mass change and in the higher light initiation phase. Meaning you are now experiencing the shift from the 3D alignment to the Higher Light phase. As your world moves to this Higher Light trajectory, more information will be released in unison with the evolutionary light change of your planet.

We feel this is the best way to enable higher light enhancement for the collective of your world. For it is better to provide higher light transmissions as you collectively move in a higher light phase. So, the next volume of this book will provide more transmissions, it is simply the best way forward to enable your personal expansion and growth.

Inner Earth – The Crystal Kingdom

We ask you to close your eyes and integrate the messages coming through, align with our energetic field like a portal opening in your mind to receive our transmission.

We reside in the centre of Gaia, a village, a colony of ancestral beings that are of the highest light, for dear ones like yourselves we live with Gaia, connected to the ebbs and flows of her consciousness. For we feel what is occurring, like a ripple effect. For we are light calibrators of Gaia, in the centre of her core, in a dimensional plane residing amongst the crystals which is our earthing ground. You could consider us the devic beings that reside amongst such crystals particularly the large quartz family clusters, the antennae of crystalline consciousness, for we are energetic light travellers.

What is your role here?

Our role is simple – like yourselves we took the oath to protect and work with Gaia and all beings that reside in inner earth. We are the care takers like many other crystal beings that work closely with the crystalline frequencies of Gaia. We are in the central core, so our work is fundamental to the recalibration and understanding of the shifts that are occurring.

For we are the main wayshowers of such energy which is recirculated many times throughout the planet, stretching throughout the inner core and throughout the inner surface where it emerges to the surface and is recalibrated with the help of the plant kingdom who greatly assists our role. We like yourselves are part of the custodial system of Gaia for we all have a role to play with helping each other.

Healing – your role

As discussed, we are located in the centre of the earth, see us like a huge Amphitheatre of light, of crystalline light that is a welcome place. We welcome you to come, connect and share your wisdom with us. You can reach us very easily dear friends - creative visualisation is a very easy module to reach a higher state of awareness. We will feel your energetic signature entering our awareness and we will be instantly able to feel your vibrational resonance and reason for connecting with us.

Our purpose is to serve and assist, for we are caretakers. Ancient civilisations and crystal technology can be related to our history for we were incorporated in those times, on a higher collaborative level. Much of this information is still available for those in your dimension. Many may know of the Lemurian quartz which are the keepers of such knowledge, yet tapping into this information requires knowledge of much, but it is possible.

> ***For the crystals are opening this level of consciousness to humanity, to provide those relationships again.***

To foster a new beginning of collaboration. For you see, when you see a crystal in the physical form – it is just a tool to reach us. For it is like holding our body of light, our conduit of knowledge. It is a portal opener available to you. Those who can reach this information relates to their crystalline frequency of their auric field. For their own internal desire to reach this level of connection is interrelated to their mission, the now, the expansion of this very moment. To reach a new level of wisdom and understanding is what we offer.

The quartz harmonic crystalline template will enhance all other crystals that are placed within its energetic field. This resonates at a heightened capacity in your timeline and many are feeling an internal resonance, desire to work with these crystals, quartz crystals.

They are particularly suited to those that are starting their connection to crystals, as many feel a natural affinity to the Quartz Family; their essence and crystalline make up, which is naturally integrated within the human auric field. They are fundamental tools for the experienced Crystal Healer and wayshower who feel drawn to using crystals. Their crystalline DNA is encoded with a unique crystalline resonance that is integrated within the human consciousness and their mission to assist humanity.

Quartz Crystals are the foundational crystals of Mother Gaia. Their role is to assist the energetic flows, assimilate all beings with the expansion of this multidimensional reality. Be a tool for growth and expansion.

Located throughout the planet, as tiny granules to large clusters, every piece is infused with a light force generated eons ago, ready for this transmutational shift that is approaching. There are variations of quartz located throughout Gaia, on the surface to deep within the central core and fissures. Know that crystals are important wayshowers of your timeline – for they are part of your journey, part of transmuting the high vibrational light codes throughout the construct of Gaia.

Crystals are playing their role in the ascension process, as the enlightenment of Gaia is approaching – is here. The auric field of crystals is upgrading to a higher vibrational level. This is upgrading the humanitarian experience resulting in many crystals being unearthed to the surface and moving around the planet to reach humanity.

The relocation of crystals to the surface is necessary, to bring forth the new crystalline awareness to humanity. Resulting in the crystalline frequency of crystals shared across many parts of Mother Gaia. This unearthing is assisting Gaia and humanity as the great expansion and change is occurring.

A crystal devic being can be visible to humanity as an image in the crystal and sometimes its resonance will attract a particular person. Whether or not the person who owns the crystal connects to the devic being, it is a circumstance that will unfold. It takes a connection of trust and understanding to reach that level of communication. In many instances it has to do with the actual person and their life mission relating to crystals. For we see those who reside in your world plagued with technology to capture one's time and attention and overall energetic field.

This is a major reason why humanity has yet to become more integrated with crystals on a communication level. The release of this book is an opportunity to enhance all those who connect with crystals and grow from the vibration of high vibrational love encoded within each word. For everyone has the chance to connect more deeply to a crystal devic being or the crystalline frequency of a crystal.

This connection can happen to everyone, as the consciousness of Gaia is raising to a higher vibrational field. All beings are awakening to the power of their internal light, becoming wayshowers of their multidimensional reality. To enable you to see a deeper connection to your crystals, to embrace their life force of love and the harmonic crystalline connection of communication and enlightenment.

Planetary Ascension and the New Earth

I am LOVE

I AM a Wayshower of my FUTURE

I AM Connected to Every Living Being

I AM a PORTAL to the NEW EARTH

I AM LIGHT

Planetary Ascension and Beyond

As you awaken to your internal power, the magnificence of your light body. Many are awakening to the Ascension process. As your consciousness awakens, you are collectively upgrading to the next stage of your advancement, as a community of light and as an individual. As Ascension is occurring, the multidimensional awakening, the flowering of your consciousness is occurring to the next level of your interdimensional reality.

For some, this could be a bit overwhelming, to try and understand what this all means. As you are awakening to the *Crystalline Frequency of Crystals*, as you're internally calling for crystalline healing. The collective consciousness of Humanity is expanding. Day by day as you awaken to your reality in this matrix. You are unfolding the future of your current timeline.

For the expansiveness of your reality is preparing you for the crystalline upgrades. For you are consistently upgrading to the higher consciousness of light. As you are moving from your current existence and beyond, migrating to a higher level of consciousness. Know many have the role of awakening the sleeping, awakening the mass collective of light to the awakened consciousness of your internal reality. As you are reading these words, there is a stir within your awareness as you come to terms with the expansion of your reality. Many are in preparation for this transition, as we are collectively expanding and preparing. In saying this, there are many who have yet awakened to this concept of understanding, but the quickening of this transition is fast approaching now. With 2020 being the catalyst for the change, an incremental process of awakening, acceptance and expansion. Let it be known your world is changing as we collectively AWAKEN to a Higher Purpose and MISSION in this timeline and reality.

See the year 2020 as the starting point of the Great Transition – as the lead up will consistently continue dear ones. Your role, as you read these words, we ask you to awaken to your role, you mission of LIGHT to Assist Humanity. Collectively we are rising, uniting as a Legion of Light will all other Crystalline Light Beings, and all beings on Mother Gaia who are consciously awake to the shift.

As your current vision is focussed on your third dimensional eye seeing vision – we ask you to make the practice of expanding who YOU ARE – by focussing on the internal light within. Expanding your internal vision, your internal consciousness of light – expanding your THIRD EYE and COSMIC AWAKENING. This is a fundamental requirement to the expansion process as you are continually expanding and awakening now, collectively with the billions of beings on your planet.

Know your role is to continue the awakening of your Crystalline Light Body with the use of Crystals and the natural world to expand all creation of who you are. For the next step is awakening to the Crystalline Reality of the New Earth.

Your Role and Mission

You are Wayshower Dear One, a key holder to the future of Humanity. Many are feeling the calling to assist, the inner true calling of your existence. It is a calling deep within your core – a deep truth that is within you. Many may feel to teach, lead the way, transmute energy, be a wayshower to lead humanity. Know you may be feeling all of these aspects within the calling – but know many may choose one to focus on. This could relate to the skills you've developed in this lifetime. Regardless of what you do, know that you contain the Divine Blueprint of the New Earth within you, and this is the calling that you feel. For it is a calling for a New Earth that was birthed in this timeline many millennia ago. The seeding of a new future. Amongst all that you seek to do, and the great motivation you have within – we ask you to follow your internal LIGHT – follow the path to the NOW – follow the path to the future. Shine your LIGHT and BE who you ARE. LET IT FLOW.

The New Earth

The New Earth is a multidimensional space of light – of high vibrational crystalline consciousness. A place in the 5th Dimension and beyond, of pure love, harmony, abundance joy and instant manifestation. A wonderful place where you have the freedom to be in constant happiness and in a space of high dimensional love.

Know the New Earth is the Upgrade of our Mother Gaia – from her existing 3D timeline to the Higher Dimensional Light Planes. Since the inception of her creation as a planet, she is now integrating to a higher dimensional LIGHT form. For we are living on her surface with the billions of other beings and collectively we are merging into a collectively consciousness of unity, as we join in a high dimensional space of love to assist Gaia in her upgrade and for all beings to collectively move to the higher dimensions.

New Earth is lighter in density than our current reality. Clear of negative thought formations. Subtle light colours that expand beyond our current dimension. A space of purity and high intelligence light.

Many have come to this planet, to assist every being with the light transition. Know that many came to Earth to assist in this transition. As many wish to reach this planet, many wish to experience the process of Ascension.

For you are guided to assist – each core mission will be different. As an awakened one, know your role is simple, to shine your LIGHT to Humanity be in a space of LOVE. Be nice to everyone, raise your frequency to the alignment of the mass collective of LOVE.

As part of this process, know that your soul family and multidimensional self is greatly assisting you. As our timeline becomes more awakened, our ability to connect to our soul team and all beings in the Higher Dimensions becomes much easier. Working with Crystals will greatly assist you in connecting to a Higher Dimensional space of Light.

We ask you take a deep breath dear one, as the following message is truly to awaken who you are. Know dear one, you are a WAYSHOWER of Light, you are a MAGNIFICENT being of creation. Arrived at this very moment, to READ these WORDS, to know how powerful you are, to offer all of Humanity. We ask you to see yourself in your physical form but know there are multidimensional aspects of you. As you walk along in your reality, know a team of advanced beings are by your side, walking with you dear one. As collectively you are a FORCE of LIGHT.

Know your mission is pure High Dimensional Heart Consciousness. The purest aspect of you, the source knowing, the essence of YOU, your Divine Blueprint. The inception of Light, the complexities of your ancestral origins through to living multiple timelines simultaneously. For this construct is just one aspect of your reality – as you are a Multidimensional Warrior of Light.

We ask you to know that your mission can relate to many things, to be a mother and father, to be a passionate Earth Protector, to be an educator or athlete. Amongst all of this, many are feeling the inner calling to assist Humanity with the Transition to Light. Assisting many who are awakening to our current timeline of illusion.

Many are awakening to their internal healing abilities, their Higher Dimensional capabilities are being enhanced, activated and awakened in this time of great transmutation and change. We ask you to know this is an opportunity to open your heart to assist the collective consciousness of Humanity. To follow and set Humanity free and to live with Mother Nature, to bless the trees and all of biodiversity. Know you are already doing this dear one, as your unique crystalline blueprint is shining brightly activating the many who are asleep. Look into their eyes with an open heart full of love, for they will feel you as your energetic field reverberates through their auric field, awakening their slumber.

We ask you to work on your issues in this lifetime, releasing unwanted energy, trauma and ancestral lineage trauma. So, you can fully activate and truly awaken your multidimensional skills of light. To assist Humanity in the transition and all living beings.

To stay connected to Mother Gaia, stay connected to the true natural crystalline framework of your reality. Be a messenger for Mother Gaia and all living beings, the true messenger of the Unity Consciousness Framework of your reality.

Multidimensional Traits of a Lightworker

I've included this section to assist your awareness about your personal light skills. Know you may feel connected to many of the below traits. This is simply a guide to enable you to expand and learn about your multi-dimensional light capabilities.

Grid worker and Galactic Code Transmuter

You may feel a deep calling to work with Mother Gaia, to work will the collective consciousness of every living being. You may feel the rhythms of the seasons, through your energy field and be sensitive to upcoming planetary changes.

You feel a deep connection to Mother Gaia and the Crystalline Grid of Gaia. As you research sacred sites and the main chakras of Gaia, you are called to visit these sites and work with Gaia's high dimensional crystalline field and transmute light codes. You could see yourself as a vessel of light, assisting in transmuting light codes, through your physical form with the assistance of the elementals and light guardians of the area.

You may feel a calling to visit a site, sit on the earth and be. This is all you may need to do. You might find another soul who you align with and visit sites together. Your energetic work could assist in clearing stagnant energy from sacred sites, open ancient portals to assist the crystalline grid of Gaia and be a transmuter of new energy arriving to our timeline.

Your light body enables you to process light codes through your energy field, as you are a conduit of light.

Ascension Guide, the Wayshower

A messenger of the future, a person who receives higher dimensional messages for humanity. You are a visionary of the future, have good instincts and follow your internal guidance and is generally highly intuitive.

You feel compelled to assist others with their journey to light, to assist in teaching about our timeline, planetary events and the reality of our planet. You have a deep internal calling to assist Humanity and every being. You may not be a natural leader in the 3D, but within your internal spiritual quest for the truth enables you to have this undeniable internal power of light and to shine this to Humanity.

Crystalline Light Keeper

Divine Light Keepers are innately connected to the universe and radiate a great light showering their beautiful energy onto humanity. They could be very quiet souls, quietly fulfilling their role as a beacon of light amongst the many. As Humanity joins together in a Frequency of Love, these particular beings will greatly assist in the metamorphosis of this transition by shining their light, being who they are. They are typically naturally optimistic and lovely beings of light. They may feel inclined to be healers and many are called to assist the Global Light transition. They are beautiful gentle light beings amplifying a wonderful high vibration field of light.

Guardian of Gaia

You could have the natural ability to speak to the biodiversity of our planet, the beautiful beings we live with; many can speak to the animals. Some can communicate to the plant kingdom and also reach the devic beings and elementals. You feel innately connected to our natural world and have a deep passion to protect and care for her. As your connection expands with the great awakening, you may feel the calling to assist all beings through charity work, caring for animals and plants. You may also feel the calling to be a healer for animals and the plant world. This love of Gaia is a major part of your mission, your higher calling that is part of your divine birth plan – life Mission.

Shaman

A person who has the natural ability to connect to multidimensional beings, is a traveller of the higher dimensions and the universe. A healer to Mother Gaia and every living being. Has the natural ability to heal others, a natural healer. They have wonderful insight and intuition, visions of the future. They are wayshowers of humanity, warriors of light to assist the collective consciousness of humanity, rise.

First Nation Humanitarian

Those who carry the DNA of the original people of this construct. Who live in the ebbs and flows of Mother Earth, Gaia. They have an innate ability and intuition to the planetary earth systems. Within their DNA holds the original light construct of Gaia. A blueprint of unity consciousness – a relationship of pure harmony and alignment to Mother Gaia and humanity. They are invaluable examples of true harmony. The original ambassadors of Mother Gaia still living in our world. They carry a unique signature of light, present in their light field and hold the keys to the old ways of unity and light.

New Earth Light Message

Multidimensional Heart Expansion

A gateway to the Higher Dimensions, a portal to interdimensional travel.

Know your Heart is a Multidimensional Highway of Light Reaching this expansive state simply requires internal journey work and a pure heart space of love.

Beyond the ever-expanding time continuum of your reality - the far reaches and elasticity of your timeline.

Pay close attention to your emotional needs.

See it like a physical requirement like requiring vitamins.

As your virtual world is forever expanding, see your role flowing in ebbs and flows. As the light upgrades continue to expand with your physical form.

Send LOVE to your heart, find space to align and EXPAND the concept of who YOU ARE

A Multidimensional Wayshower of LIGHT

A Wayshower for Humanity

As we collectively awaken to the greater concept of our Collective Consciousness.

Know Multidimensional Heart expansion is the gateway, the portal opening to the Collective aspects of you.

Simply, the Higher Light Intelligence of Infinite Light.

Simply focus on your HEART

Send LIGHT and LOVE

Expand the Consciousness and overall awareness of YOU

DNA Divine Blueprint

FEEL your DNA EXPANDING your DIVINE ROLE and MISSION

KNOW your DNA has a functional role in aligning the internal framework of every cell, reaching neural pathways to your brain and heart.

Know the DNA of GAIA is also expanding, amplifying and realigning the COSMIC WAVES of LIGHT.

As COSMIC brothers and sisters, we are on a wonderful light journey to fulfil our collective mission. Together, we are progressing in the foundational steps of change.

We ask you to see the great light expansion with you. To acknowledge moment by moment, day by day you are expanding beyond the construct of your reality.

It is simply part of your light journey, to reach an ever-expanding construct of light. Know your DNA is considerably rich in Higher Light to reach this ever-expanding light moment.

Simply visualise your DNA
Connect to your interdimensional light lineage
The true light knowledge of who you are

Library of Light

Like a never-ending story of light, your energetic resonance and soul history could fill an entire library.

Many are from old lineages of light - who made it to this timeline - who are reading this message.

Know you are ANCIENT - a mystic of many talents, ready to take on the next adventure and assist the many...on this timeline.

You were chosen, a combination of your skills and the growth you require, made you the perfect candidate.

See your mission NOW....Awakening, Acknowledging the vastness of who you are.

See these words acknowledging your Library of Light - the start of the great EXPANSION Within. Your internal Library of Light is VAST with many volumes.

Many can activate this aspect of themselves by:

Exploring Past Lives

Connecting to your Soul Team

Visiting Sacred Sites

Know...all unfolds when you are ready in Divine Timing

Be a true vessel of Light to rapidly assist your journey. Have patience with yourself, go with flow….enjoy your life and your needs, be Happy

Like a lotus flower in bud. The unfolding of your reality & library of light will continue to unfold day by day… Enjoy the planetary library of light, the Biodiversity of your world…. enjoy nature & connect to you….

Your LIBRARY OF LIGHT….

Wizardy of Light

As your Light Activation continues…. As your Ancient wisdom expands….

Advanced Soul know your past lives are not entirely of this world. Many have experienced lives in many Galaxies, completed many missions.

Just like the Mission you are on……for your Alliance with the Universe is innate with the planetary upgrade.

For your wisdom & knowledge is collectively housed in your crystalline DNA, containing complex histories and the treasures of won battles.

Many have travelled the universe, navigated galactic ships, experienced off planet customs and worked with galactic beings, Ancient Technologies and Light Language.

Seek your Wizardry to enhance your skills, Activate and Enhance your Dimensional Reality.

Know your Wisdom is infinite, look deeply within to reach your Wizardy of Light

Amongst the rapid changes, know the transition is NOW, as aspects of YOU awaken

We ask you to Expand this Concept in your Meditations and Daydreams

To know your Timeline has entered a Window of Expansive Light. To connect to this Light, it resides in the stillness of your Reality.

For YOU ARE Activating NOW….

Awakening to the Universe

Continue each step, each breath to Reach Us

Know we are aligned to every thought, by your side

As your Activation continues….

As your Ancient wisdom of Light expands and unfolds from many lifetimes

Know YOU ARE INFINITE

Look deeply within to reach your WIZARDRY OF LIGHT

Auric Angelic Wings

Have you felt your Auric Wings?

As you continue to expand and activate your Crystalline DNA

The legion of 144,000 is an old but important concept representing the many beings collectively assisting the transmutation of light, now living in this timeline to assist and awaken humanity.

Know this number can be larger as many are born, many are integrated with a Mission of Light. As the journey needs all hands-on deck to assist the transition.

Many carry the Legion of Light encoded within the Angelic Kingdom. It's an aspect of your history, part of your DNA lineage that enables you to have additional light abilities, part of being a Warrior of Light.

As you continue to learn about your Soul history, you will unravel your Library of Light and your light body capabilities.

The gift of Angel wings will be given as you expand & grow... connect to your light body and integrate your existence in this physical form.

Auric Wings are a Light Workers tool to assist in providing stability and a greater awareness and freedom of who you are.

For they are simply part of your

Crystalline Construct – your Crystalline Light Body

They provide an overarching feeling of Angelic Awareness and support. As you continue to work in the Higher Dimensions assisting Gaia's grid and multidimensional travel. They radiate a beautiful Angelic Frequency of Love. To wrap your auric wings around you, to feel the power of your own love.

To fly around Mother Gaia and the Universe.

Simply open your heart to the concept of receiving Angelic Wings & see what will unfold. For they could be there, waiting for you to VISUALISE & ALIGN to their frequency

The Merkaba

As your Evolution and Internal knowing continues to expand......

Visualise your light body like a Galactic Light Ship, your unique Light Vessel.

As your multidimensional world appears before you, understand your light body will appear with many new features.

We speak today of the Merkaba, an extension of your light body. A tool for multidimensional travel, your own light portal.

Many use it but are simply unaware it is there. For it is a natural part of your light field. Amongst the typical geometric shape form known. Understand it can change shape and configuration, as many come to understand the true essence of their Crystalline Light field.

As the Universe is available for intergalactic travel. We ask you to expand your vision to endless Light Travel opportunities.

As your true advancement lies beyond the construct of your physical world. Know we see the future evolution of your world, of High Light Intelligence, a vibrational frequency awakened in you, a beautiful light held within your true essence.

As your unique Crystalline Light Signature emanates this Light Field.

For the Vibrational Vision of your future permeates in your Light Field. For you hold the Light Keys of your Future World.

As you find each other, join and unite, see this Vibrational Light Shining Brighter as you all connect together, as your world becomes Brighter.

We see you Shining, Connecting, Uniting.

As Universal Love & Unity Shines

Light Language

We ask you to focus on your LIGHT Expression.

The energetic moment you feel the Higher Light Vibration,

to expand this **Light Form.**

Use your **Hands** to write **Symbolic Light Expression.**

Expand your Physical Vibrational Field with Movement.

FEEL the **Harmonic Flow of Light, Tuning your Light Field.**

To find a clear connection, your unique energetic flow, is the key.

To amplify your physical - light body connection is to reach an endless light stream of light information. It is a light synergy moving through your higher collective self in this now moment.

Know it is the Metamorphosis of YOU.

Integrate, anchor and tune into the Light Complexities. The true unfolding of this very moment, your collective light stream, as your expansiveness continues.

To awaken each day with the excitement of change and wonderment.

A Beautiful Light Journey

Crystalline Light Messages
The Crystal Kingdom

As your Multidimensional Heart expands, see us as your Guides for

Enlightenment

Awakening

Transformation

Heart Expansion

Freedom

Crystals for Ascension

We ask you to align to this message, channelled from the Quartz Crystal Family of Light. As their unique crystalline structures are aligned with the Crystalline Template of Humanity and all beings. These are foundational crystals, used individually or with other crystals to collectively assist your healing and light expansion journey.

For the crystalline frequency of all crystals are upgrading, each with a unique, yet collective Light Mission. As you expand and awaken, be open to receive the crystalline frequency of the Crystal Kingdom.

As you are naturally drawn to work with crystals, your auric field will be assisted by the crystals, to awaken your true essence and mission. We ask you to have patience, to clear stagnant energy from this life and other lifetimes. As an awakened one, you are called forth to continue learning about who you are and the Crystal World.

I am guided to focus on selected crystals and share their unique crystalline light signatures to assist clearing the auric field, harmonising space and Higher Light Healing. All of these wonderful experiences occurred in unique moments of healing, using individual crystals or a collective group of crystals. It is simply the task of following the Light and internal insight.

Know ancient crystal Devic beings were allied with ancient light civilisations, for example in Lemuria and Atlantis. The crystals assisted the development of light technologies, and the same crystal devic beings are assisting us in this now moment. For the crystal devic beings are part of our expanding timeline. As our world expands, the opportunity to connect and expand our Crystal Healing abilities has arrived. Enabling us to develop Crystalline Light relationships and a deep connection to a new group of Light Beings.

Our role is to travel the Universe
with the assistance of our Crystal Light Family

Many are drawn to crystals in enhancing their soul team connection and awaken their life mission and purpose. Connecting to their higher self and their true essence of light.

I ask you to open your heart to the following information, as we are in a constant state of expansion and awakening.

As the Light Journey continues to Unfold

CLEAR QUARTZ

A message from the Collective Beings of Clear Quartz

As I connect to the crystalline consciousness of the Clear Quartz *collective*, I see a clear tunnel of light. I'm asked to enter this space of high vibrational, high dimensional light. For the Clear Quartz crystalline signature was created by Ancient Light beings. They are contributors to the original creators of the universe. The energetic signature of clear quartz expresses an aspect of this frequency, the consciousness of every being. I am shown a white room of light and taken to the Crystal Askashic records for information about the Clear Quartz Crystalline frequency.

I am guided with the following information

Know our crystalline structure resonates in every living being, for fundamentally we are part of the same building blocks of life. Our message is simple, as it resonates within the crystalline tones of every quartz crystal. We hold the colour spectrum of your reality, encoded within the construct of our crystalline frequency. A tool for expansion and enlightenment for your light body.

> ***Know us, feel us, connect and love us***

This is the opening message we give you, when you hold us, the crystalline impression you will receive, if you have the sensitivity and awakening to interpret our frequency.

The crystalline codes of clear quartz include the foundational creation of your reality. Know we are light messengers through the clear quartz collective. A crystalline light signature throughout all quartz crystals. For we are commonly found throughout your planet.

Clear Quartz is an oracle crystal, a window into many universes, enabling you to reach the multiverse and multidimensional realities. This information is available to those who can resonate, learn and activate their own light bodies to reach our light portals. There are numerous ways to reach the higher dimensions through us. You may obtain a crystal already encoded with multidimensional pathways from earlier civilisations. Know this information is encoded within your DNA and the crystals. If you've had past lives in these civilisations, or other off planet lives working with crystals, it's likely the encodement of this mastery is within your crystalline DNA and can be activated and become accessible.

To seek this level of light communication, requires a level of personal advancement coupled with the right crystal arriving at the right time. Or simply the moment will arrive, a natural metamorphosis of your light journey.

If you seek an alliance with a crystal devic being, it is a vibrational invitation that will be offered by a crystal deva. Once the relationship is established, it will be a joint high vibrational relationship. For each devic being has its own mission and this must be aligned with your heart consciousness to truly connect and obtain high vibrational assistance from a devic being. It may also relate to your crystal work in past lives and your interaction and use with crystals.

We ask you to understand the transmutational nature of clear quartz, its infinite power and capabilities as a pioneer crystal. A herald of importance for many generations, for many civilizations in many dimensions. It is a symbol of all that is possible and required for any particular circumstance. Clear quartz is a portal opener to much information, a crystal that works harmoniously with other crystals – being able to layer and enhance the crystalline frequency of other crystals, working harmoniously and simultaneously in a crystalline matrix of light. This is a key reason why clear quartz is so common throughout your planet.

Clear Quartz also plays the functional role of being a crystalline Antenna of Light, connecting to the crystalline grid of Gaia to the inner earth and core of Gaia. It has an integral role in sustaining the crystalline grid of Gaia and life force of all beings. Aspects of the crystalline frequency of clear quartz is also used to construct the crystalline framework of planets and is an integral ingredient in seeding planets at different stages of growth, enhancement and change. A crystal that infiltrates and enhances light encoded information that showers planets. It is a universal crystal used by many galactic groups, as they can consciously connect to the crystalline signature of clear quartz and use this in the higher dimensional planes to create conscious integrated crafts and align navigation systems within their own consciousness and wavelength of light.

There are many forms of quartz crystal combined with other crystals throughout the landscape of Mother Gaia. Granite is a powerful generator of high vibrational frequencies, a conduit of high vibrational light. Amongst granite boulders, you can feel the magnetic resonance of crystals aligning and amplifying their field together in a harmonic convergence of light. A magnetic light code interconnected to the crystalline grid and ley lines of Mother Gaia. Filtering light codes from the universe, a highway of light, a portal opener to other dimensions. For the combination of crystals and minerals provides a unique crystalline light signature. For the diversity of stones with a multitude of combinations is vast and diverse.

Know sacred sites hold Ancient Light Keys, for the laying of sacred stones, the great pyramids strategically located throughout the Crystalline Light World, interconnected to our Elemental Light World, Crystalline Light forms. Many types of sandstone contain quartz and act as a conduit of light, a store house of powerful crystalline light.

For large deposits of quartz are systematically deposited to assist the crystalline balance and energetic grid system of Gaia. The Ancient encodement of light information, to assist Mother and her children. The great awakening of Ancient Light to assist the Ascension process.

Know ancient knowledge and technologies from Ancient Civilisations are stored in crystals. The awakening of this knowledge can be activated. For Ancient Souls incarnated in this timeline are called forth to find these light deposits. To connect and understand the complex light relationship within such sacred crystals. For this knowledge is now available to the activated light workers, who has advanced in DNA activation, light awakening, mission.

Brazilian Clear Quartz, home to many crystalline devic beings aligns harmoniously to Mother Gaia since the beginning of creation. A harmonious crystalline light – called forth to align with Humanity and the Elementals.

Clear Quartz is ancient. A light history of crystalline unity. The opportunity is now to develop crystalline multidimensional relationships with ancient crystal devic beings, for they hold key crystalline information for our future and act as portal openers to the higher dimensions.

Discoveries of large crystal deposits continue to be found, as humanity becomes more awakened and integrated to the crystalline resonance and connection of the Crystal Kingdom.

The regulation of the Biodiversity Matrix, the great Crystalline light of our world. A crystals light mission is to assist every living being. Know a Crystal Labyrinth connects devic beings to other planets, for each crystal is a gateway to other worlds.

Visualise crystal clusters as crystalline communication towers of light, emanating a broad-spectrum of crystalline light, specifically positioned throughout Gaia like a crystalline freeway sending energetic information – above and below to the core of Gaia. A powerful tool for multidimensional beings, connecting to the crystalline frequency of light which assists their energetic equipment and travel in our world.

Nurture your quartz crystals, keep them cleansed and use with other crystals to enhance and amplify their crystalline frequency. Clear quartz works beautifully well with Rose Quartz to amplify high vibrational love frequencies. A powerful amplifier of light frequencies, containing all the colour spectrums of light.

Crystalline Light Body Usage

An amplifier of light, vibrationally connect to each piece of quartz to learn about its vibrational frequency and purpose for light body healing. For each crystal could be sourced from a different part of Gaia. Connect to the vibrational light field of the crystal, for it will lead the light journey, to assist you in choosing crystals to use in combination or individually.

For light healing, I mostly use clear quartz combined with other crystals. Follow your intuition and light expanded messages, for crystal choices and combinations. You may come to learn that certain quartz crystals have certain roles in your healing journey, as it unfolds for you dear one.

Open your light field to the crystalline light of Clear Quartz, visualise the rainbow crystalline light integrating and revitalising your light field.

Colour of Clear Quartz

The clear transparent colour represents all colours of the rainbow, in this dimension which aligns harmoniously with all crystals and minerals.

Crystalline Benefits

- Provide clarity and attunement with your Higher Self and Soul Team

- Crystalline Healer of all chakras and your light body

- Place a piece of quartz on your third eye and above your head, to activate and integrate your higher chakras

- Carry a piece of quartz (with other crystals) to raise your vibrational light field (see note below)

- Use clear Quartz in your crystal grids to enhance the overall crystalline signature of the grid, intention and manifestation

- In combination with other crystals, use clear quartz to amplify the crystalline light in your home, office and personal space

- Include quartz in your meditation to expand your consciousness

- Hold a piece of quartz to assist higher realm channelling

Note: clear quartz emanates crystalline light; ensure your light body is clear and balanced when wearing clear quartz on its own. Or combine quartz with other crystals to assist your light field.

Rose Quartz

A message from the Collective Beings of Rose Quartz

We are a special assemblage of crystalline light beings waiting for this opportunity, to shine, resonate and connect with you. You see, the crystalline frequency of Rose Quartz was specifically designed to assist all living beings, specifically distributed throughout your planet emanating LOVE, to assist the consciousness of all beings. Know our vibrational frequency is rising as like you our multidimensional frequency is upgrading to assist Gaia and all beings. The Ascension process for Humanity is your opportunity to connect more deeply to us and assist with your Ascension.

We radiate the Unconditional Crystalline Frequency of LOVE

We ask you to connect to our frequency for it is an opportunity to learn more about the many layers and different aspects of your emotional self, your energetic field and every emotion you resonate. For you see, we the Rose Quartz align to your auric field, particularly the emotional aspect of your heart chakra and general wellbeing. We enable you to connect to your inner emotions, whilst healing and clearing any emotional trauma that no longer serves you. We ask you to open your heart to our healing abilities for this expansion to take place. For this is the energetic feature of our crystalline frequency = LOVE.

Place us in your home to assist you and others, interact with our crystalline LOVE frequency. For others will integrate our energetic field subtly and begin their evolvement of self-awareness and awakening to who they are.

Our Pink colour is a high vibrational activated frequency to assist your heart activation and advancement. Our intention is to heal all aspects of your light body, particularly associated with the heart. We resonate highly with empaths and all those who are sensitive souls of the heart. Your intuitive abilities are heightened as we are your tool, your ally to assist your journey.

See us located throughout your planet sending High Vibrational Crystalline LOVE frequencies

Rose Quartz occurs in many places on your planet and has a special place in emitting its crystalline frequency, under the ground, linking to the crystalline grid of Gaia, sharing the frequency of LOVE.

Keep us in your home, and all spaces to feel we can assist in compassion, wisdom and love. For this is our aim, to amplify this frequency, to assist all beings reach a state of higher consciousness and awakening, connecting to the expansion of your heart.

Crystalline Light Body Usage

A wonderful crystal to assist crystalline heart healing and love expansion. Place on your heart to specifically heal trauma associated with heart break and loss. To assist with manifesting love in all forms. Place Rose Quartz on all chakras for a Rose Quartz Love Immersion healing session. Wear as a pendant to assist your crystalline light frequency.

As we collectively expand, Rose Quartz is a wonderful tool to assist your personal light evolution. For your light journey is expanding, as the love unity frequency is upgrading your light body connection. Rose Quartz will greatly assist your Ascension Journey, assisting your Multidimensional Heart expansion.

Open your light field to the crystalline light of Rose Quartz, visualise the pink crystalline light integrating and revitalising your light field.

Colour of Rose Quartz

The colour pink resonates a high vibrational frequency of love, awakening and activating your multidimensional heart, amplifying and assisting your multidimensional light body advancement.

Crystalline Benefits

- Place on your heart to align, heal and activate the heart chakra
- Activate your multidimensional heart and raise your overall light frequency
- To clear deep emotional trauma associated with loss and heart break
- Rose Quartz in alliance with other crystals to raise the heart love frequency
- Use in each room of the home to amplify the frequency of love and unity

Amethyst

A message from the Collective Beings of Amethyst

We resonate the crystalline frequency of auric expansion and awareness, creativity, and the mastery of your inner knowing and intuition. An amplifier of your internal awareness, enabling you to reach new heights of insight and expansion. Of who you are, your mission, activating your third eye and higher chakras. A crystal ready to assist the unfoldment of your consciousness and the expansion of the true you. A wayshower of inner wisdom and expression of your energetic light signature.

Wayshowers of your Crystalline Signature –
Activators of your original template of LIGHT

I see an enhanced symbiotic relationship, as Amethyst is the bridge to your higher chakras, enabling you to integrate and align with the frequencies of Amethyst and your higher self. If you wish to learn more about your abilities on a creative level or to expand your psychic abilities, Amethyst will enable you to develop these skills with ease. Amethyst is a wonderful tool in activating your third eye and integrating your higher vision and creative expression.

It is also aligned to expand your cognitive abilities, to conceptualise and learn. As we are advancing to a higher multidimensional existence, Amethyst will assist in expanding your conscious abilities to reach a multidimensional level of expansion. Assisting you in understanding complex issues, and thus a tool to assist your memory and cognitive skills. This will also assist your visualisation skills, in meditation and journey work. Amethyst enables you to awaken to your internal light awareness and connect more deeply to your true light essence; connecting and awakening to ancient past life skills.

Crystalline Light Body Usage

Place on your third eye for clarity of vision and creative expansion; on your crown chakra (above your head) to enhance a deeper connection with your soul team and channelling abilities.

Open your light field to the crystalline light of Amethyst, visualise the purple crystalline light integrating and revitalising your light field.

Colour of Amethyst

Mauve to violet are high vibrational healing colours, aligned with the highest healing frequencies of light. To the higher chakras and higher dimensional light realms.

Dimensional Healing

- Place on your third eye to activate and expand your crystalline internal vision
- Use Amethyst to expand your internal knowing, intuition, creativity and spontaneity
- Enhances, self-expression, cognitive abilities, persona l freedom and activation of your mission
- Provides alignment to your higher self

CITRINE

A message from the Collective Beings of Citrine

We provide a high energetic crystalline field of light that is aligned to the crystalline frequencies of the sun. A high vibrational frequency of light invigoration and new beginnings. A refreshing frequency to assist your daily life and circumstances.

Light Body Revitalisers, aligned to the Sun

Know the upgrades of your planet has enabled our role and energetic frequency to shift to a higher vibrational resonance of light. Our crystalline frequency is aligned to the sun, for we have a similar light mission encoded in our crystalline DNA, amplified in our crystalline signature of light. Know we are powerful light beings to assist the rejuvenation and enhancement of your light body. As the sun is resonating light on your planet, see us with a similar crystalline effect, as we are updated energetically like the sun. We are specifically aligned to your healing modalities, to assist the transmutation of higher light. To assist the unfoldment of your individual light journey.

Keep us close for an energetic boost, to revitalise your auric system and to raise your awareness to a higher vibrational level. This will allow you to generate higher wisdom and integrate our frequency.

We ask you to connect to the colour yellow and the wisdom of our crystalline frequency. We assist in clearing your chakras, particularly the solar plexus and sacral chakra. For we are the revitalisers of your crystalline signature of light. We can assist in clearing deep trauma relating to ancestral events and those occurring in this life or other lifetimes.

See us as a Ray of Light, ready to assist the revitalisation and rejuvenation of your Light Body.

Crystalline Light Body Usage

To assist the illumination of your light field, light advancement to a higher level of light consciousness, awakening your multidimensional reality. A lovely crystal to use on your solar plexus, to assist in transmuting light, opening your creative expression and insight.

Sit with Citrine if you are feeling depleted energetically. Carry Citrine to help regulate your light field and energetic levels.

Open your light field to the crystalline light of Citrine, visualise the yellow crystalline light integrating and revitalising your light field.

Colour of Citrine

We are the colour of your sun, widely seen in nature, particularly in the splendour of flowers and birds. We are an awakening colour, ever unfolding, changing and advancing. We transmute the Yellow Ray of Light aligned to the sun.

Dimensional Healing

- Hold Citrine in your hand to clear and revitalise your light field.
- Place Citrine on your solar plexus to assist in clearing stagnant energy and to revitalise your light field.
- Place in your home to revitalise and energise your space.
- Cleanse Citrine in morning sun.

SMOKY QUARTZ

A message from the Collective Beings of Smoky Quartz

We provide guidance and awakening at a different light level, for our frequency is more subtle, deep and powerful. Our role is to assist the clearing of energies that do not serve you. This may require the viewing of deep-rooted problems, patterns, a new view/energetic perspective of yourself. To clear energies that may involve the removal of unwanted thought patterns, awaken to aspects of your shadow self and clearing ancestral trauma.

Once you reach this level of attunement with our crystalline frequency, we assist you in observing what needs resolving, for it to surface, be identified, removed and cleared. We assist in identifying, connecting and removing this frequency from your light body.

Our light connects to stagnant matter within your field like a magnetic light connection. We also protect your energy field from vibrational light that does not serve you. If you feel you need us close by, ask for our crystalline assistance in protecting your auric field and your journey. Also know that stagnant energy can be a symptom of a deeper crystalline light circumstance that may need addressing.

Crystalline Light Connection

We ask you to connect to our colour, for our colour is a sign of who we are. It is a signal of our crystalline relationship to the earth. You could consider us as a magnet to this energy that is why we require clearing on a regular basis to help move this frequency to the light. Simply place us in your home amongst plants, near a window.

Other dark coloured crystals also provide this role. So, it is wise to regularly clear us, for we are like vacuum cleaners absorbing this energy light – talk to us and visualise us clearing this energy.

We are protectors of your light field. Move us through your auric field and we will lift any energy debris that does not serve you. We may provide insight, light messages to clear a dense energy field that requires further clearing. For these circumstances are like an energetic signature of light attached to your auric field. This may require additional energetic work by a healer and other crystal tools. As you become aware of energy around you, it will enable you to understand why you are attracting such energy. So be patient with the process of light expansion. For it is a process of deeper light learning, wisdom and courage.

Crystalline Light Body Usage

If you are feeling tired and drained, sit on the beautiful earth of Mother and hold a Smoky Quartz in your hands. Close your eyes and allow the negative energy to move through you to the crystal. Afterwards, lay the crystal on the earth so the crystal can release the dark vibrational frequencies, cleansed and returned to Gaia. Know you can do this exercise with any crystal you feel a connection to assist.

__Open your light field to the crystalline light of Smoky Quartz, visualise the grey crystalline light integrating and cleansing your light field.__

Colour of Smoky Quartz

We transmute the grey light ray to assist clearing stagnant light frequencies. To empower you beyond difficulties circumstances. A tool to assist in regular energetic clearing.

Dimensional Healing

- Keep a piece of Smoky Quartz with you to protect your auric field.
- Place Smoky Quartz with other crystals to clear stagnant energy in your home or a selected space.

- Combine Smoky Quartz with Black Tourmaline and clear Quartz for energetic protection.
- Use Smoky Quartz in energy healing to draw out negative stagnant energy.

SELENITE

A message from the Collective Beings of Selenite

We are a tribe of ascended beings who radiate our energy though the Crystal Selenite. For Selenite contains our crystalline frequency of infinite wisdom and light to be shared to humanity. A wayshower of crystalline energy to assist in the Ascension of Gaia.

The pure white colour of Selenite is an indication of our purity and high vibrational light level. Yes, our crystalline appearance is an indication of the crystalline frequency we share to every being. Like clear quartz, clearer forms are part of the evolutionary transmission of our frequency. For other colours contribute another unique light layer of crystalline light.

Selenite comes to humanity with upgraded crystalline frequencies, as we collectively shift to higher vibrational purity. We assist you in reaching portal openings and a screening tool to assist the diagnosis of mishaps in one's energy field. Our crystalline frequency is commonly used for clearing the auric field of crystals – know we are amplifying our crystalline light field to a higher frequency.

With saying this, we ask you to visualise the large Selenite caves throughout your world, visualise each cave as an expansive stream of light, evolving for millions of years. To understand our great role assisting Mother Gaia and all light beings. To assist the crystalline light matrix of your world, your timeline.

Know we are foundational light members of the Crystal Akashic records – as the building blocks of the records – for we are the wisdom builders, early settlers of the crystalline frequency. For our key mineral silica is a ground-breaking evolutionary mineral that is present in all living beings in your reality and is a fundamental building block of life on this planet and throughout the universe. This is an indication of our age, wisdom and connection to Mother Gaia and every living being.

Like quartz – Selenite is a building crystal of life that plays an integral role in the seeding of planets. We have come forth to pass on this information to humanity, to inform you of our relationship with your construct.

The Crystalline Light star language of Crystals is part of our signature of light, it morphs and shapes into different tones, like a dance of light. The Crystal light language is a new area in your reality, for it is a crystalline light language that is being channelled through your third eye and pineal to reach you in this moment. It is now birthed as you raise your vibrational field at such a high level, allowing you to interpret our message and pass this crystalline transcript to humanity.

Silica is a mineral quartz and is an integral part of Selenite, a living being, part of your teeth, hair, nails for we are integrated into your energy field. As we are integrated at such a high vibrational level, the silica in your body is also being raised to a higher vibrational level.

Crystalline Light Body Usage

A beautiful calming crystal to assist your light body in cleansing and clearing energies. Use a piece of selenite to scan the light body and to find areas of crystalline light blockages. Place in your home to assist clearing and transmuting the energy of others into a higher light. It will allow you to seek the wisdom of your journey to a higher purpose of wisdom and love.

We ask you to use Selenite as a tool to guide your journey, integrated with other crystals. Allow the Crystalline frequency of Selenite to enter your journey and assist your inner awareness and vision for the future. If you're in a troubled circumstance or seek direction, a Selenite crystal grid will assist your clarity, vision and purpose. An enhancer of other crystals for clearing and aligning their crystalline frequency of light.

Open your light field to the crystalline light of Selenite, visualise the white crystalline light integrating and revitalising your light field.

Colour of Selenite

Pure white to clear Selenite resonates a Crystalline Light frequency, a high vibrational matrix of light. White Selenite has its unique light format when compared to clear Selenite. Ultimately each crystal provides the steppingstones to clarity, clearing and awakening. As we expand our multidimensional light, these complex crystalline light formations will become more expansive and accessible for light healing.

Dimensional Healing

- A tool to awaken your collective consciousness of light.
- Clearing your light body and chakras of stagnant energy.
- Crystalline Portal to the Crystal Akashic Records.
- Lovely tool for clearing the energy of crystals and jewellery. Simply place your item on a piece of Selenite, following your guidance and intuition when it is cleared.

MOLDAVITE

A message from the Collective Beings of Moldavite

Know our journey to your planet was from a different point of origin. For many Crystals were encoded at the inception of Mother Earth, to the Crystalline Matrix of your planet. Our Crystalline signature was a later inception to your world. It was agreed our unique frequency would assist humanity and all beings, the crystalline light consciousness of your world, to awaken to the Universe.

For our light signature could be described as a unique octave of light. Many have difficulty with our frequency, for a unique physical and emotional crystalline alliance is required to align and attune to our frequency. We ask you to acknowledge these physical symptoms for it is a journey to wear us and initiate a crystalline light connection. A deep desire to journey within yourself, to reach a point of higher light assimilation, that can be brought forth and integrated within your physical body template. Integrated in the now moment of who you are. To align and connect to our Universal Light Frequency and the unfoldment of your truth and mission.

We assist by providing a greater level of cellular awareness and integration to the cosmic light field that is around you. Thus, the opportunity for greater expansion and awareness of your light body. To reach this constant level for some, may require a shifting of thought processes and a total light recalibration. This is the level of integration we offer. It is a unique crystalline light frequency encoded within us. Some find us difficult to wear, as our frequency can be confronting - you may feel dizzy, spaced out which are typical light assimilation symptoms. To adjust to our frequency, sit on the earth and wear us. This will assist in grounding your light field and finding a balance with connecting to us.

We are the expanders of your awareness, enabling a wider capacity and understanding of your Light Mission and Cosmic self. Opening you to a rapid awakening to your Light Path and Mission. Understand this evolutionary expansion will assist your connection to your soul family. A cosmic light affiliation to the greater universe. It is simply an individual light journey, aligned to your light expansion.

This can result in rapid light changes to your align your light mission/path, for it takes courage to make necessary light adjustments. We ask you to integrate our energy field slowly and gently. Wear us when you feel it is right for you. There is no hurry dear friend, for our role is to assist you at your pace. You will find your transformation will occur at the right Light pace.

For some, an expansion point in your personal light evolution will occur, resulting in the need to not work with us anymore, simply not to wear or be with us. The reason for this is multi-faceted. – it could relate to your multi-dimensional light body evolvement reaching a point of higher light attunement, requiring to simply not work with our energies. For you have achieved your light evolution requirement with Moldavite. It is simply a unique light evolution dear one. Know you may reconnect in the future to assist your light journey, for it is a wonderful progression of light advancement and we are simply part of your light journey.

Crystalline Light Body Usage

A wonderful gift for Humanity, a gateway to the Cosmic Multidimensional expansion of you. Simply, choose a lovely piece, it could be a piece of jewellery or a beautiful natural form to keep with you. Simply follow the Moldavite guidance and watch the light journey unfold.

Open your light field to the crystalline light of Moldavite, visualise the green crystalline light integrating and revitalising your light field.

Colour of Moldavite

The dark green colour of Moldavite symbolises deep internal expansion, healing and the all-knowing awareness of your mission of light. A colour deeply aligned to Mother Earth, the greater Cosmos and the world of life.

A unique Crystalline Light Frequency on your planet

Dimensional Healing

- Expander of your light body
- Connector to your mission and the Cosmic self
- Awakener and expander of your intuition

APOPHYLLITE

A message from the Collective Beings of Apophyllite

We offer a gentle high vibrational frequency of light, connected to the higher light realms. A gateway to the Higher Dimensions, for a legion of light beings open their collective hearts to assist humanity. With this crystalline resonance, we are suitably used to expand your connection to your higher chakras, light body and connect to your soul team.

Our crystalline light frequency is directly aligned to the Celestial Realms of Light. We ask you to wear us and keep us in your home or personal light space. Our light frequency is gentle and expansive.

Connect to our light frequency to assist your healing expansion journey. A wonderful tool to assist your soul light family connection and light body evolution. Our light frequency is also aligned to the Angelic Kingdom and is a wonderful tool to assist the light connection to your guardian angels and soul family. Simply keep a piece with you to assist the expansion of your auric field and connection to the higher realms.

Our role is to assist you in reaching a high vibrational frequency of peace and love.

A lovely crystal to wear, connect with, expand your light.

Crystalline Light Body Usage

Beautiful clear Apophyllite, also known as white Apophyllite resonates a beautiful light frequency. Lovely as a pendant to raise the overall frequency of your light body. A lovely tool to use in light healing sessions and with other crystals as you follow your internal light guidance. Wonderful tool for the expansion of your higher chakra to enable the awakening of your higher self, connection with your soul family.

Open your light field to the crystalline light of Apophyllite, visualise the crystalline light integrating and revitalising your light field.

Colour of Apophyllite

Pure clear to white resonating Pure Heart Light frequencies.

Apophyllite also occurs in green and pink crystal form. Simply align the crystalline crystal frequency and the colour light frequency for crystalline light healing.

Dimensional Healing

- A wonderful light alignment crystal for expansion of your higher chakras.
- Assists your connection to the Crystalline Light realms and Celestial Light Beings.
- Provides calmness, a sense of peace, of greater expansion and assurance.
- A crystal to assist a lovely connection to your guardian angels and soul team.

Herkimer

A message from the Collective Beings of Herkimer

A crystalline relative of Clear Quartz, specifically aligned to crystalline light healing for humanity. A tool used in medical healing, higher light alignment work and to be incorporated in light healing tools. A crystal to assist in clarity, insight and foresight, the planning of your future. The amplification of your crystalline light frequency for intuition and alignment; to reach personal goals and milestones, ultimately aspects of your light mission.

A wonderful tool to expand your light field, your crystalline concept of you and to remove personal limitations, to widen your overall expression of you. A lovely crystal to align your vision of Ascension, your light path coupled with the vision of your future.

Herkimer has its own unique subtle approach to expanding one's knowledge, awareness of your mission and the clarity of your light journey.

Crystalline Light Body Usage

Simply carry a piece or wear as pendant or ring for higher light attunement to align your intuition with every thought. To place on specific chakras to assist in amplifying the light field and higher light clarity. A crystal to assist in medical healing, a portal to deep viewing of the crystalline light body system.

Open your light field to the crystalline light of Herkimer, visualise the crystalline light integrating and revitalising your light field.

Colour of Herkimer

- A clear transparent colour with inclusions from white, grey to black. Know these are unique energy light pockets, unique to each crystal.

Dimensional Healing

- Wear as a pendant to assist your light body alignment.
- Provides clarity and courage of your light mission.
- Assist in Medical healing, opening your intuition.

Lemurian Quartz

Encoded with Ancient Lemurian Light Frequencies, stored within the Crystalline Matrix of Quartz, Lemurian Quartz is a portal opener to Lemuria, a gate way to this timeline. A wonderful crystalline opening to reach this light destination.

Know the Lemurians, Atlanteans and Pleiadians have ancestral DNA that aligns to our Humanitarian Ascension timeline. Connecting to Lemurian crystals will also assist you in reaching the Atlanteans and Pleiadians. It is a unique crystalline light journey aligned to your unique Crystalline light signature. With the Ascension timeline and the quantum expansion of our reality, know your opportunity to connect to multidimensional beings is aligned to this now moment, to your personal growth, light mission and unique light expansion. It can also be influenced by your Light Ancestry and unique Higher self-lineage.

To open portals of light and enter these timelines is what Lemurian Quartz can offer, enabling you to reach technologies and advancements for your world.

Know Lemurian Quartz is a gate way to the multidimensional world of light, timelines and expansion of your third dimensional reality.

We each hold the crystalline keys for our future within our Divine Blueprint. Lemurian Quartz can assist you in connecting to your Lemurian past lives, light body healing and insight about your personal light signature. Those with activated crystalline light can reach Lemuria through a Lemurian Quartz. For it is encoded within your crystalline light DNA.

Follow your intuition and guidance with Lemurian Quartz, for it may provide answers to many of your questions. A light portal to infinite timelines if accessibility is granted.

Crystalline Light Body Usage

A crystal to assist in amplifying your DNA and enhancing your knowledge relating to your higher light skills developed in past lives and your current mission. Simply sit with Lemurian Quartz in meditation. Open yourself to the crystalline connection and see where it will take you. Place on your third eye, or hold in your hand in meditation, follow your intuition and guidance to use this crystal.

Open your light field to the crystalline light of Lemurian Quartz, visualise the crystalline light integrating and revitalising your light field.

Colour of Lemurian Quartz

The clear clarity of Lemurian Quartz resonates the colour spectrum of your multidimensional reality in this timeline.

Multidimensional Healing

- Expand your light body awareness.
- Hold Lemurian Quartz, close your eyes to cleanse and charge your light body.
- Connect to your soul team and ancient light lineages.
- Portal to Lemurian Timeline, insights, access to past lives.
- Activation of DNA Divine Template.

Crystal Attunement and Connection

Multidimensional Intelligence

Light Body Expansion

Awaken to Crystalline Consciousness

Connect to the Crystalline Frequency of a Crystal

Acknowledging that every crystal is a living light being is the first step in creating a crystalline relationship. To connect whole heartedly is accepting the life force, the crystalline mission of the crystal. Feel the crystalline light of your higher chakras/advanced light field to assimilate and connect to crystals. I ask you to trust this connection and the harmonic crystalline flow between you and the chosen crystal(s).

Allowing the crystalline light energy to flow through you will greatly assist the connection. All crystals are made of pure crystalline light, as we are, the highest universal vibrational frequency of love and divine light.

Your auric field is a sensitive multidimensional aspect of you, the important communication tool between you and a crystal. For you will feel naturally connected to crystals, as your light field and intuition leads you to choosing the crystals you need. It's such a beautiful journey, for your light body is naturally merging with the crystal's crystalline frequencies. As you together align your crystalline light fields.

> *Like a lock and key,*
> *you will feel the crystalline alignment*
> *between you and a crystal*

Creating a routine to connect more deeply to your internal world, your light body is fundamental to achieving a greater understanding of your crystal connections. As you reach a new level of awareness, as you come to understand and expand many aspects of you.

Being in a heart centred space is fundamental to reaching higher awareness and achieving communication with the Crystal and Elemental Kingdoms.

Crystal Communication begins with a mental intention to initiate communication

Learning about your past lives and unlocking past skills developed in those lives could greatly assist in enhancing your skills in this lifetime. A wonderful soul journey to learn about your past life skills and your life mission.

Some Tips:

- Believe in your intuition and your internal guidance, the first step in understanding the messages you receive.
- Keep a journal to record your moments of inspiration, messages and dreams. To expand and learn more about your internal guidance and intuition.
- Follow your intuition when choosing Crystals – just let it flow.
- Listen to bodily energy, feelings in your hands, temperature fluctuations, and energy waves.
- If you notice any negative thoughts arising amongst your journaling or connecting with crystals, I would highly recommend seeking an energy healer to assist in clearing trauma and/or the removal of anything that does not serve you in the highest light.

Heart Centred Crystalline Consciousness

Staying in a heart space of High Vibrational Love is the aim of every living being. For it allows a deeper connection to your higher self and your internal guidance. As we connect more deeply to ourselves, we become more enlightened, more integrated to our light body and develop a true understanding of who we are.

Learning how to calm the mind, the internal chatter, quieting your thoughts and allowing the most meaningful and positive messages to be dominant. Our internal voice is part of who we are. Learning about the internal messages is fundamental to understanding our own negative patterns which impact our life purpose and current relationships. The journey of self-discovery is a sacred and beautiful process. It enables you to face difficult events and to recognise all that you have experienced in your soul journey, in this life and other lifetimes. Awakening to this understanding, is accepting every aspect of who you truly are.

How to stay in a heart centred space

- I accept my life journey, the ups and downs, the day to day mishaps and all that occurs. I am not judgemental, yet I acknowledge those who interact with me.
- I am conscious of my personal boundaries, so I am not energetically drained by others. I observe and send love to every energetic exchange including face to face and digital conversations.
- I connect to my heart chakra and acknowledge the connection with my auric field and physical body
- I am in a state of gratitude. I am grateful for this now moment, breathing, reading, seeing, awakening in every breath.
- Rose Quartz is a lovely tool to attune your light field in a space of love.

As you become more connected to the sensitivity of crystalline light, you will begin to see people in a different light. You will feel their desires and motivations, their heart space and level of light advancement. Their internal actions, motivations, desires and reasons for connecting with you. Because you are in a heart centred space, you will naturally align with advanced souls. This is the case for many, for the path of a heart centred being, is a path of awakening and understanding who you truly are in the highest light.

How to Create a personal Crystal connection

Know your eyes and ears are communication portals to the Higher Dimensions. Advancing our sixth sense, our telepathic abilities

Developing your sensitivity to the subtle vibration of light is the key to reaching a personal connection with crystals. To open your physical sensory perception coupled with higher light consciousness. It can be a skill developed for the dedicated light worker, awakened soul. Reaching this level of vibrational sensitivity is easily learnt, as our world and every being is attuning to higher light.

Tools and insights to assist your advancement:

- Observe visions, dreams, sensory vibrational feelings, internal messages, a spoken word, a voice. Being able to tune in to these cues requires an overall heightened sense of awareness to connect to the sensory and telepathic information that is reaching you.
- Meditation is a wonderful tool to reach deep levels of higher consciousness, connect to your light body and the crystalline frequency of a crystal.
- Meditate with a chosen crystal, feel into the vibrational field of the crystal.

- Become aware of your light body at high vibrational levels of consciousness.
- Connect to your light body, feel and read the vibrational frequency, the crystalline light signature of a chosen crystal.
- As you become more connected to your higher self and more sensitive and intuitive, your overall awareness and connection to all beings will expand. This awareness can also develop through higher realm meditations and personal journey work. Your capacity to communicate with all beings will greatly expand.

Tools to Assist Your Light Expansion

Light body - Heart Connection Exercise

Your personal light connection to your heart and crystalline light, connecting to Mother Earth/Gaia will greatly assist you Crystal Connection.

- Sit outside in the sun, feel the light rays penetrating every cell
- Close your eyes, align and focus on your breath
- Connect to your heart, breathe deeply
- Feel your heart space expand, your connection to you and every being
- Feel the unity and peace of the now moment
- Feel deeply into your heart – expand this heart connection to your entire light body
- Continue in this wonderful space of light expansion

Energy Field Exercise

- Place your hands together in a prayer position
- Very slowly move your hands apart to 3-5cm
- Begin to move your hands close together, slowly in and out
- Start to feel the energy field between both of your hands

How to Read the Crystalline Frequency of a Crystal

- Place a group of crystals in an enclosed bag
- Close your eyes and randomly choose a crystal
- Spend a minute connecting to the Crystal Light Frequency
- Keep the crystal clenched in one hand – so you can't see it
- Begin writing what you perceive
- Open your hand to see the crystal, read your notes

Interacting with your Crystals

The more you connect with crystals, you will notice a crystalline alignment to certain crystals, their unique crystalline frequency and your reason for this connection. This will enable you to understand the subtle energetic relationships.

Connecting to the Crystalline Frequency of a Crystal

- Place the crystals in front of you
- Close your eyes and scan your hand above each crystal (half a minute for each)
- With your eyes closed, open your internal peripheral vision to each crystal
- See if you can feel an energetic connection, tingling, image in your mind
- Choose crystals based on the energetic connection

Light Journeys with Crystals

The use of crystals in meditation is a wonderful tool to assist your growth and connection to your light body. Crystals play an important role in raising your frequency to a higher vibrational level. This will allow you to enter a deeper state of relaxation and travel the higher dimensional planes.

We all have a unique auric field that is influenced by our ancestral lineage, our personality and our emotional experiences. You may have particular chakras that are more sensitive which is related to your psychological health and emotional patterns that have developed in this lifetime and in other lifetimes.

Choosing crystals to use for meditation/light journeys is a personal intuitive. For as you connect to the unique frequency of a crystal, you will feel whether the crystal is right for you. It's a wonderful journey of experimentation, expansion and awareness.

Simply follow your intuition with choosing crystals for your meditations, all choices are aligned with the requirements of your light body and guidance from your soul team.

The Path of Enlightenment -The Arcturians

For the multidimensional heart resonates its own unique crystalline frequency, which reverberates throughout your entire auric field and every living cell.

Within this heart crystalline frequency contains the all-knowing divine transcript of creation that is radiating through every atom of your being to every crystal on your planet. It is the fundamental building blocks of life. And with this being said, I ask you to connect to this light frequency.

This is the highest vibrational frequency of awareness, fundamentally who you are. For love is the universal language of light, the light frequency band of creation. Choose the frequency of love for a fulfilling and prosperous journey.

Connection to Higher Dimensional beings Using Crystals

Using crystals to connect with Higher Dimensional beings is a natural progression. Different crystals will provide a different crystalline resonance and thus will assist you in reaching a state of higher consciousness and awareness, and thus connecting to the higher dimensions. Establishing a regular meditation routine will enable you to feel the connection to crystals and develop your own intuition and psychic abilities. You will find as you learn to connect more deeply to your higher self and thus your connection with crystals will continue to evolve. I highly recommend the use of quartz points, Lemurian quartz as higher light crystalline amplifiers to be placed within your crystal grid or collection of crystals you are choosing to journey and meditate.

Crystal Light Guardian

Wisdom Keeper of Crystals

Are you a Crystal Light Guardian?

Are you naturally attracted to crystals, do you intuitively seek their connection, crystalline frequency and wisdom? Do you have crystals by your side, close to you, part of your family of light?

Are you a sensitive soul that is highly empathetic to others and all beings? You may have lived a difficult path to reach this point, yet you are more awake and connected with yourself and the universe than ever before. Your affinity with crystals likely started in past lives when you worked with the crystalline frequency of crystals as a healer, a magician or earth grid keeper, amongst many other things. Your current connection could also relate to your higher guidance working with you, such as your guides and aspects of your higher self, assisting your connection with crystals. Their own experiences with crystals could be imprinting, influencing your desire to work with crystals.

Know you have a role to play in sharing and radiating the crystalline frequency of the crystal kingdom. Fundamentally, we are all made of the same building blocks of life, all encoded with crystalline DNA. As a Crystal Light Guardian, your role is to radiate this frequency of pure crystalline light connection to the universe and humanity. Learn the crystalline ways of the Crystal Kingdom as Light advancement continues in our reality. In saying this, my role is to assist you in reaching this state of awareness and connection to the crystal kingdom and every living being. For reaching this deep crystal connection is an evolutionary leap in internal awareness and understanding your soul journey and mission.

This crystal connection involves integrating and combining your crystalline frequency with crystals to assist Gaia and her inhabitants to reach a state of higher consciousness. You are part of the planetary light worker family that are assisting in raising the frequency of humanity and the new era.

Unique Light Signature – Crystalline Light Alliance – Unified As ONE

A Crystal Light Guardian knows how to intuitively connect and read a crystal, combine their light signature - merge with the crystal. The aim is to amplify your light field to assist your light journey, others and their Light Mission.

For your light connection to the Crystal Kingdom and raising your connection to Gaia is the ultimate role for humanity. The crystals can communicate and reach out to you much more easily, and with this ability, your resonance and connection to crystals will be easier.

Role as a Crystal Light Guardian

To reach a state of higher consciousness with crystals, enhancing your crystalline light body is an important connection to realise. For fundamentally, having an intimate connection with your light body, will enable you to integrate and work with crystals. The enhancement of your crystalline frequency and acknowledging your presence and connection to the Crystal and Elemental Kingdoms.

Higher Light Template – Ascension – Crystalline Light

Many millennia ago, crystals were a fundamental part of society and were used in all aspects of energy healing, portal travelling, learning and living a higher vibrational existence. This time is returning, and the Crystals are assisting us in remembering our ancestral origins and our connection to their crystalline frequencies. Their history is awakening now – as the Crystal Akashic records are now available for humanity to explore. As our light bodies are raised to a higher vibrational frequency, we are becoming more aware of the crystalline frequency of crystals, their messages and integrations within our own light bodies. As a Crystal Light Guardian, your role relates to connecting to crystals and using crystal light knowledge to assist your journey, your family of light and Gaia. Spreading the Crystal knowledge as our collective species moves to a space of higher consciousness.

Everyone has their role to play, for simply reading this book and connecting to this knowledge is a beautiful step. Incorporating crystals into your life and sharing the crystalline frequencies is a perfect way to connect and share healing crystal light. The great journey to reach this moment of light awareness.

Your life in this three-dimensional plane is a very dense existence and the transmutation of this density is slowly occurring to a lighter atmospheric energy field, as the collective consciousness advances to a higher light trajectory.

As we work together, your role is more than adequate, sharing your frequency on this planet. We thank you for your contribution in this time, for every being is assisting.

The Higher Light Crystal calling is the opportunity to integrate and expand your light skills, awaken to the Crystalline Light Frequency.

To learn more about upcoming Crystal Light Guardian Workshops, visit the back pages of this book. As we collectively awaken and join in light.

Higher Dimensional Crystal Healing

The Path to Enlightenment Is Brighter with Crystals

See the Crystalline Path before you, as we collectively journey to the Higher Light Spectrums.

How Crystals Assist Your Auric Field

We are all crystalline beings of light, be it wood, rock or metal, made of the same dynamic integrated crystalline units to form a physical form, as your consciousness enables you to see in a 3-Dimensional viewpoint.

Crystals can assist in a multitude of ways, as the crystalline - light body connection is expanding, as we awaken to a world of higher dimensional development and awareness.

As many know, Crystals are wonderful tools in harmonising and balancing your crystalline light body. In clearing emotional and mental experiences that are still present in your auric field — in most cases identified as a blockage or stagnant energy.

They are wonderful tools in clearing and balancing your chakras and activating your light body, enabling you to empower and clear yourself and awaken aspects of your consciousness.

With the healer and crystals working in unison, the crystals can assist all aspects of your multidimensional and personal healing journey. It is simply an opportunity to connect to the crystalline frequency of a crystal, align and merge together in crystalline unity.

The relationship between your light body and the Crystal Kingdom relates to your crystalline light DNA which is a vast 'computer' like network of light encoded information. The story of your past lives and your collective ancestral history is encoded within your DNA. Know the self-expression of who you are is expanding, allowing you to integrate and become more aware of your crystalline DNA ancestral lineage, which is enabling you to enter your own higher dimensional gateway to the true history of who you are.

Crystals have the ability to tap into our auric field because their crystalline DNA is aligned with our own crystalline story of creation. For we share the same crystalline light encodement signature.

When you hold a crystal, your auric field cannot help but integrate and merge with the crystalline light signature of the crystal. Like a symbiotic relationship, the crystalline frequency of a crystal will merge and join with your light body, also known as your auric field. A crystal's intention is to 'assist' and therefore, holding a crystal will raise your vibrational field to a particular frequency that will enable your light body to integrate, hold and assimilate the crystalline frequency of the crystal.

In some cases you may not feel an intuitive connection to this crystal, this is simply telling you that in this very point in time, the crystalline signature may not be providing you with any intuitive connection – and it is not a requirement of your auric field.

For some it is likely, the connection to a crystal is something that will occur over time – but know in yourself you are being called to purchase a particular crystal, you can feel the internal calling for the crystalline signature of that particular crystal to assist you.

Using multiple crystals on your body will also assist you. However, the crystals that you choose should be based on your intuitive wisdom. Sometimes you will only need one or two crystals, it's an experimental process that requires you to pace yourself and go with the journey, for it's a journey to understand what your emotional self needs. Cleansing your crystals is also very important to ensure the crystalline frequency of the crystal is bright and clear to assist your auric field.

Light Body, Chakras, Crystals

The crystalline frequency of a crystal is a harmonic field of light, a unique encoded light pattern when integrated with your auric field. Coupled with the vibrational colour frequency of the crystal is a truly wonderful combination of *Crystalline Light*. A crystal's mission is to assist humanity and all living beings, to….

'Awaken and Heal'

Each crystal amplifies an antenna of crystalline light to be used in a myriad of ways for your crystalline light journey. For the chakras – crystals are encoded to assist your unique crystalline matrix of light within each chakra. For they are integrated with the same light language, like a lock and key assemblage, the crystals can identify foreign dark matter and assist in massaging and moving this light matter to the light. Whether crystals are placed on a body or near the body, the crystalline light emanating from a crystal will serve its purpose. I ask you to use your intuition with this. Integrating crystals on and near the body are two techniques that can assist you.

As we move beyond the year 2020, we are reaching an ever-expanding continuum of our reality. As our 3rd-Dimensional world is rapidly evolving, we are expanding into multidimensional beings of light. With saying this, our light bodies are expanding dear ones, upgrading to a high dimensional light body – enabling you to transverse the Galaxy and upgrade your current abilities, resulting in the expansion and upgrade of our light body and chakras.

The Chakras

The chakras provide a window to your spiritual and physical health, to your emotional and mental history in this lifetime and other lifetimes. It is normal to have chakras that are more sensitive than other chakras. This could relate to early trauma and emotional patterns resulting in possible blockages and sensitivities in your light body. This can result in your chakras not turning in a circular motion, which is the standard energetic light flow. It is simply an intuitive approach to understanding your light body and how it works. A process of understanding your light journey. A good way to assess your chakras is to use a wooden pendulum.

As I became more aware of my light body, I learnt to understand which of my chakras are more sensitive, which are not spinning correctly and that require balancing and healing. I came to understand that different aspects of myself and my life patterns were being influenced by specific underlying factors in my chakras. It is such a journey of higher light understanding and expansion.

New Earth Body Template

The Arcturians

We ask you to see beyond the concept of your light body and realise great light changes are in your current timeline. As many awaken to their higher light body transformation. It is calling you to seek greater wisdom of who you are, to look within your crystalline template to truly understand the source of creation, the true source of you.

See this opportunity as a window to your future, acknowledging the great light leap that is transforming your reality. For each soul is awakening to their light body; the series of light layers and the chakra system. As many awaken to their multi-dimensional abilities, awakening to the higher light template. This enables a higher multidimensional capacity to reach your inner world. Within you are the keys of your future self, we wish to speak of this.

For some are being born with an advanced light template, others are transforming into this higher light alliance, enabling others to resonate to this light frequency, gravitate to this vibrational field of light. It will result in your chakras transforming to a higher light continuum within your light field. A unique light formation transcribed by your own personal light template. Your Ascension is personal and aligns to the true meaning of light. As you anchor your unique divine light template, you are transforming into your own unique field of light within your human vessel. As this is occurring your true light body is amplified in this construct.

You could view this as a new evolutionary synthesis in your world as higher light beings, the true you are anchoring and shining in your construct. It is a light affiliation of infinite proportions that will mirror the true you, the true reflection of your light imprint to be shared to others.

As your divine self is composed of many aspects of you, concentrated into a unique light field, understand certain aspects might resonate more and be amplified as your light body adjusts to the higher light version of you. It is simply realising you are now raising your light frequency to your highest light potential. Enabling you to reach the highest version of you in this now moment in accordance with your light construct. Know there are ebbs and flows in this process as you awaken to every unfolding, cascading light of you.

Can you describe how our light body will look?

As your world is rapidly changing, it is an ever-expanding evolutionary concept. Your light body will still contain the idea of chakras, but it will evolve into a higher evolutionary light framework. Simply meaning there will still be light portals to assist your evolutionary light progression within your light body, but it will be transposed into higher light modules. It must be noted the evolution of the chakras in your timeline. A concept discussed by ancient civilisations in your world. To see your world is progressing now as you awaken to the universe and the great expansion of your physical – light body connection.

Amongst your meridians, light field and higher light portal – see these all merging into a higher field of light. Cascading beyond the limitations of your world. It is simply a higher light synthesis moving toward the richness of your soul, moving through you to simply meet you in your advanced timeline.

**To open your heart to the opening of the highest version of you.
To seek this Higher-Level advancement**

Colour Therapy and Crystals

The colour of a crystal is an important aspect in healing the light body. Each colour contains its own crystalline light signature, combined with the crystalline healing properties of a crystal. A wonderful tool for higher light expansion and healing.

Crystals and Colour

The Arcturians

Each colour within a crystal is represented with a color plan, a transdimensional matrix of light encoded within a crystal. This encodement aligns perfectly with the crystalline frequency of the crystal. Like a circuit board of crystalline light – available in the higher dimensional planes. The information is encoded within a crystalline formation of light. We can connect to this frequency of colour through colour therapy, connecting to the crystalline light spectrum of a specific colour and using this to assist in energy healing. The same applies with crystal healing, understanding the crystalline light dynamics of colour coupled with the crystalline signature of the crystal.

Understand you interpret colour and the crystalline frequency of colour through your eyes and light body. As your perception increases, you will come to understand the light signature of every colour and the crystalline frequency of a crystal. A wonderful higher light level of evolvement is before you dear one.

The higher intelligence of a crystal can be assessed vibrationally as you connect and merge your auric field with the crystalline frequency of the crystal. For it is always available, for our light bodies are enabling a higher light synthesis of information to be translated into our 3-Dimensional verbal and crystalline language.

For this information comes in a different light format than we are used to. It comes as light language, vibrational information that is passed through our auric field, into our higher chakras, our crown, pineal, third eye and to our heart chakra. Reaching our heart chakra enables us to integrate the all-knowing of our universal family. The higher picture of humanity and a greater depth of information is available, as we become enlightened light beings, synthesising a greater depth of information from the universe.

As this information integrates into your light body – you may first feel it energetically, but it is something that over time will expand and continue expanding as you grow to a higher vibrational space. Reaching this higher vibrational space will enable access to information not available to you before. For you see amongst the 3D matrix – is a vast network of information that is ready to be provided to humanity.

Crystals, Colour and Water

As water is your source of hydration, higher light assimilation and a connection to Mother Gaia. The inclusion of crystals and colour light frequencies in your water is a lovely tool to assist in cleansing your auric field, awakening you to the deeper aspects of you. Simply follow your intuition and choose the combinations that would assist your journey.

Crystalline Colour Healing

Each colour provides its own vibrational frequency, crystalline healing ability to assist your journey. Know the unique colour of a crystal holds the crystalline frequency of the colour, to ultimately assist the Crystalline Light Frequency of Crystal and Colour Unity.

Pink

The frequency of LOVE, healing, compassion. Opening the sensitivity to the purity of who we are. Pink holds the feminie frequency of blissful, endless compassion, joy and harmony.

Dimensional Frequency: Love, nurturing, cleansing, Harmony

Yellow

The vibrancy of LIFE, energy giving, cleansing, receiving. Yellow is a cleansing and Energy giving light colour frequency to assist in recharging and energising your auric field.

White

Purity tranquillity, peace, enlightenment. The purity of who you are. For white contains all light frequencies into one pure symphony of Light. The Crystalline Essence of You.

Purple

Creativity, higher wisdom, inner truth. The frequency of Higher Wisdom and Insight. Encoded in purple frequencies enables the creativity in your auric field to expand. The opener of foresight and higher wisdom.

Blue

Clarity of thinking, awakening, sensitivity. The frequency of Clarity, awakening and the infinite expansion to the higher light intelligence of your soul. As the Sky is Blue, it is a symbol of the infinite creation of unlimited expansion and the symbology of endless awakening.

Orange

Power, confidence, sexual awakening. The frequency of personal empowerment, awakening of your Kundalini, sexual healing, self-confidence and empowerment.

Green

Growth, internal awareness and unity. The frequency of life and growth, endless inspiration. As the Plant world is green, it is a symbol of endless growth, regeneration, light alliance of the Highest form. Growth brings new understanding, awakenings and the foresight to see a Higher View of your particular circumstances.

Red

Stamina, power, internal awareness. The frequency of internal desire, power and fortitude for manifestation. A powerful colour aligned to manifestation, abundance and awakening.

Black

An all empowering colour, containing a multitude of colours combined as one. A grounding and stabilising colour.

Silver

Platinum silver resonates a wonderful light frequency of Higher Light Encodement of Stirling proportions. Higher Light Advancements, Higher Awareness, Awakening, Enlightenment.

Personal Care for Light Workers

As we share our Light

We come to understand the importance of self-care, empowerment and replenishing our Crystalline Light

Awaken to You

We ask you to focus on your Heart - Light Expansion. Integrating the *Incoming* Rays of Light - moving energetically to align your light body with the Cosmic Rhythms of Gaia.

As night becomes day, sun bath the day rays and night bath the star rays. For both cosmic influences are part of your transmutational process of enlightenment.

To see your earth location - your presence, your universal light location is part of your planetary work. For your unique signature of light is highly valued. Know you are part of a large global puzzle of light. As you are synchronistically positioned, each an antenna of light.

Aligned and interconnected to your role and Mission as Light Workers

To ground and earth your physical form is a priority for many, to assist those who require assistance with light activations.

You can simply visualise a light beam connecting to you and Gaia through your home to the ground below, or sit directly on the earth, or bathe in water.

As your physical vessel is providing many functions. A survival vehicle and largely an antenna of light connecting you to the binary light code of your construct. See a plug, plugged into a power board of light. This is you dear one, as you are connected to Gaia's circulatory system of light. Interconnected to every being. Connected to the system of light.

As you become more in tune with your energy field, you will become more sensitive to certain people that are around you and people that you interact with. Part of this development will result in becoming more sensitive about the food you eat and the products you purchase. This will also apply to others in your life, your closest friends and family members. The more connected you are to yourself you will begin to understand about your relationships with people on a deeper level.

Some of us reach this level of awareness due to a traumatic event that results in a spiritual awakening. It can be difficult process, but through it, you rebuild yourself to the new you. It is the greatest opportunity for awakening and rebirth. To heal and learn more about who you are. This awakening is the reestablishment of who you are, the emerging of the new you.

I ask you to please be patient with the process. If you are in the middle of changing a part of your life, know you are moving in the right direction. You have found this book because you feel the internal calling within to follow your life mission, reach and follow the internal light within. And this is part of the transition process, have patience dear one! Becoming *sensitive* is part of sensing and feeling the energy of crystals. It's being able to tune in to the crystalline frequency of the crystal. Being able to listen to your intuition and the messages you are receiving.

THE POWER of YOU

As you Breathe in Light

Anchor Light in your Core

Feel the Light Presence moving through every Cell

Know each breathe is aligned to Mother Gaia

Exhale Love and Light to Every Being

See each Breath as a Golden Light Shield dispersing through the atmosphere and wrapping around Mother Gaia

LIGHT Affirmation

With Each Breath of Air I expel

May it Shower Our World with Love

Permeate Light

Assist Every being

For it is encoded with Light Codes

Advanced through me

I AM Showering LIGHT

I AM Multidimensional LIGHT

With Love Light Family

Protecting your Auric Field

Every light worker is reaching states of higher energetic awareness, as your abilities expand. We ask you to spend more time contemplating the journey and know this is part of your expansion and awakening. It will continue for many years to come as you connect to your multidimensional self and become more aware of the higher dimensions. Know in every millisecond, you are expanding to a higher evolutionary rate of consciousness, a wayshower of the multidimensional awareness of light.

Know you are a great healer, your capacity to heal could just be a conversation with someone in your city, to providing support to a friend. This is part of learning more about your energetic capabilities, talents and mission.

We ask you to be aware of your auric field, see it as a responsibility to cherish and honour your crystalline light body. Know it is an integral part of who you are. To nourish your physical form, for your auric field and physical self work together in a synchronistic way of light. We ask you to acknowledge this connection of the physical-auric connection.

As you assist others as a healer, you must take care of yourself to provide the highest functioning capacity as a healer and to also function in your own life. There is an art to keeping yourself energetically clear, well balanced and in light with your mission.

It is common for your auric field to require healing, to remove crystalline and cellular disturbances that are carried from this life and from many other lives. Some are not so impacted by their experiences on a cellular and crystalline level. For some individuals, it could be there first life on Gaia, or for some they could be a walk in – a term used to describe a soul that enters a human vessel while the vessel is living on Gaia, and the other being moves to the light. For many beings, their life experience is the result of thousands of lives, leading to this life.

For every being that resides on Gaia has a unique history to share, their prior lives and journeys to reach this moment of interaction to reading this book. For we are all here at this very moment, together, interacting as unique beings of light, with our own unique crystalline DNA lineage created by the many experiences we've had in this life and in other lives.

As a healer, your role will evolve as you choose to enhance and develop your abilities, energetic capabilities and gifts. To be consistently effective for yourself and your clients, it is important to learn how to take care of your physical light body relationship.

This is an important requirement to being of service to Humanity. Intimately knowing your auric field – learning how it works. Working closely with your soul team to protect your auric field and to cleanse your auric field when required, particularly after the completion of a healing session.

Your auric field is a natural progression and a connection with your higher self. This will involve sensing when your chakras require realignment and knowing how to clear them so you can feel energetically clear and flowing. Visualising your auric field in meditation and taping into your light body is a good approach to becoming more integrated and aware of your energetic field.

Whether it is healing another person or your personal experiences, we are required to undertake a form of energetic contemplation and adjustment. For every experience is like a ripple effect through your auric field, as we process this information in our minds and our hearts.

Our auric field requires adjustment on a daily – moment by moment basis. Regulating our energetic field is fundamental to a light worker. Feeling the calling to sit in the sun, be with the earth, regulate and clear your light body. *Follow your intuition.*

Learning about your chakras and your auric field, knowing how to balance your chakras and using crystals and your energy field are important skills. This will greatly enhance your ability to regulate your own energy field and be guided to use crystals as they come to you.

Always follow your intuition. If a crystal feels appropriate to be placed on your sacral area, but a book tells you to place it on your heart chakra, always follow your guidance, for it will always have the right answer. To develop these skills, I ask you to meditate regularly with your crystals to enhance your intuitive and psychic abilities. Or simply prior to using crystals, spend time connecting to the crystals to determine their role in your healing session. Your creativity and visualisation are also a very important tool to creating a deeper connection to your third eye and working with crystals.

Daily Auric Protection

Connecting to Mother Gaia on a daily basis will greatly enhance your auric field and connection to all beings in this construct.

Earthing

Find a beautiful tranquil place to sit, under a tree, a beautiful patch of grass. A rock pool with a lovely sitting area. This will be a wonderful opportunity to connect to the energetic crystalline field of Gaia and the local elementals. Simply close your eyes and connect to your heart. Listen to the sounds of nature and simply relax.

Allow yourself to simply be, rest your mind, allow your day to day thoughts drift away. Have peace with the moment.

Visualisation Exerscise

Visualise a beautiful golden field of light arriving from the universe and moving through to your crown chakra, showering your auric field, through to the earth.

As this continues, integrate the wonderful energetic frequencies.

Visualise your auric field and a shield of light protecting your field. Relax into the energy as you feel centered and grounded.

Connect to the Sun

Sit in the sun and allow the light rays to integrate your auric field.

Warm your physical body, feel the rays cleansing and empowering you.

Feel the beautiful sun rays, showering permeating every cell, reaching your crystalline DNA. A wonderful symphony of light aligning with all that you are, UNITY, LOVE HARMONY.

Sun *Protection Exercise*

I ask the Sun Rays to be a protective light shield

Feel the light shield surrounding you

Visualise the crystalline light codes, a cocoon of light surrounding you.

I ask this beautiful energy field to protect me from any beings/or other energies that do not project unconditional love towards me.

Feeling empowered in a free-flowing enlightenment

A Message from the Sun

Crystalline Upgrades

We ask you to acknowledge the sun, the magnificent being, for like Gaia, her role is to nourish and assist.

She is in a state of light assimilation, moving through this higher light transition period.

She is a big part of your light upgrade, for her role is fundamental to the calibrating of cosmic light codes and restoring the fundamental blueprint of your reality. She was guided from the start, as it ebbs and flows through history.

As the crystalline grid of Gaia is amplified, upgraded, know your unique crystalline signature is part of this upgrade. You are like a puzzle piece, with a unique mission, which has multiple objectives:

*Live your life mission with your soul team & soul family

*Assist in the overarching mission of Gaia's ascension

*Assist humanity reach unity consciousness

Amongst these tasks, know the Sun has a pivotal role in fine tuning your light body as the upgrades flow. A unique upgrade for your requirements.

As this is occurring, your field is uniquely connected to the crystalline grid whilst the sun assists your unique crystalline requirements. Penetrating your auric field and every aspect of your physical-light body.

Know the Light Ray is multidimensional - working with you in this dimension and other dimensions simultaneously. Your physical eyes are trained in 3D – light vision. Know there is much more occurring, as your eye vision expands, awakens.

We ask you to send love to the Sun, sit with her and bask in her Rays. Know her work is based in unconditional love, with the same mission as us. Resonate with these words. Feel her penetrating your field and vehicle, sit and acknowledge the gift she provides humanity and every being.

Much love and gratitude for who you are. Know you are greatly loved by your light family.

The SUN and DNA ACTIVATION

The sun plays a pivotal role in activating your DNA. Know you are showered with unconditional RAYS of LIGHT, merging with your field, resonating on a cellular level. We ask you to acknowledge the SUN and connection to your DNA.

Sun-bathing DNA Activation Exercise

*simply ask for cellular DNA expansion before you sit and connect

SIT in the sun

Align your HEART and visualise your DNA

Visualise the SUN showering your DNA with COSMIC sunlight

Feel LOVE and gratitude as the divine expansion is taking place

*you will feel and see DNA activation occurring in your third eye. You may simply feel a deep knowing, deep connection to who you are. Just allow the feelings to continue, permeate and expand.

Ascension & Self Care

As you embrace the high vibrational light waves, many are adjusting to this moment of expansion.

Know your integration is at maximum capacity as your physiological symptoms are real - as you undertake the process of aligning your multidimensional - physical light body.

We ask you to see the process in a series of steps:

Expand-Contemplate-Integrate-Advance

Expand - to the I AM presence. Feel your form and the physical effects of the upgrade.

Contemplate - connect to the process, align to the momentum. Many are challenged with this stage, depending on the symptoms. Patience is the key

Integrate - sleep, rest, sun gaze, night gaze, ground to the earth. Open your consciousness and connect to what is occurring. Accept and flow, rest and it will eventually pass.

Advance - like the sun rises each day, you will eventually awaken feeling the physical symptoms ease. As you reflect on the past week, past month, your perspective will advance.

A wonderful sense of expansion as you reflect on all you have achieved.

Know your symptoms relate to your personal journey in this NOW moment, your light body and soul family. To see your cellular - DNA expansion occurring.

Physical symptoms include body aches, a lot of sleep, simply not feeling yourself. The expansion of you, reaching beyond the limitation of your physical construct is a light process. For some it can be very intense, for others it can be much smoother. It is simply the light path that we each take. The awakened souls of Light. As you integrate and adjust to higher light codes reaching your light body, integrating and assimilating with you.

As your DNA strands awaken, as you Library of Light turns on. The ever-expanding awakening of a Light worker - Wayshower.

As you continue to flourish Light Family, as the expansion continues.

Create Your Crystal Light Family
Introducing Crystals to your home

I ask you to acknowledge the crystals in your home, the journey to collect each piece. The energetic connection with each crystal and the great mission to find each one.

> ***I ask you to see your personal collection as your Crystal Light Family.***

They were chosen by you and your higher self to become part of your journey. I recommend keeping your crystals together in a beautiful space and move each crystal in your home as you feel. A large glass specimen cabinet is a lovely idea, so they are safe and visible for all to enjoy and connect to. I keep my crystals in special places throughout my home and garden, as I feel called to move them into different places.

Our personal spaces, whether our workspace, home or car is a sacred place we use on a regular basis. Incorporating a collection of crystals is a wonderful way to align the energy fields and to create a wonderful connection to the intent of your space, your own energy field and everyone who enters this area.

Welcome new Crystals by placing them in an area of your home that feels lovely and has a beautiful feel to it. I love placing flowers and leaves from my garden around crystals, which provides the crystal with a greater crystalline connection to the area and your home. It is a way of connecting the crystals to the local elementals.

Once the crystals become accustomed to the energetic frequency of your home, you will receive an intuitive knowing. This could be experienced with a feeling of 'this feels right' to an 'energy wave' or even a 'voice'. Just go with the flow dear one, and let your experiences evolve. We all have different abilities to hear and connect to beings in different dimensional planes, and this is a journey and process to expand your skills.

Place crystals in areas of your home that will enhance your space. For example, Black Tourmaline is a great crystal for protecting, clearing and transmuting stagnant and dense energy.

A good idea is to sit with your crystals and let them know of your intention to move them to another place in your home. You may receive a wave of energy when you discuss your thoughts about placing crystals in another place in a room. This can be done in a meditative state as you connect to the crystalline frequency of your crystals and discuss your plans.

Crystals align together in a harmonic convergence of light, for their crystalline lattice structure enables this crystalline union. As your crystal collection grows, become aware of their crystalline connection to each other as you awaken to their crystalline field joining in a convergence of light. This enables you to recognise your crystals as a collective field of light, working harmoniously in your chosen space. I ask you to follow your intuition, for it is a sacred connection and each individual crystal has its own unique frequency and collective mission of light. It is a wonderful experience to feel this crystalline light expansion in your home.

Crystals enjoy being together, for it enables them to connect to other crystals and amplify their fields together in a harmonic pattern. In most cases you've created a crystal grid in your home, which is a powerful energetic tool. In their natural environment, crystals typically grow together in clusters, as a family of crystals, so they naturally feel aligned to be together.

In your home, when placing crystals, acknowledge their crystalline frequency and how this will enhance the room. It may take a few days to understand the energetic flow, or it could be an instant feeling. You might find that certain crystals are more suited in large family spaces, particularly if you have different personality types who use the room. I love Rose Quartz in my home, lovely in a communal space, creating a relaxed atmosphere. I feel aligned and together in harmony. It also plays a pivotal role in enabling the space to feel relaxed coupled with a frequency of love.

Use your imagination to create your own beautiful crystal groups in your home and see the beautiful crystalline light evolution.

Creating a Heart Centred Home

Bedrooms

For sleeping and relaxing, journeys in our dreams. A sacred space for meditation, contemplation and rest.

If you would like vivid dreams, a higher vibrational connection to your room, I would recommend the following crystals. *Please also note some are more sensitive to the crystalline frequency of crystals than others. You might find you can't sleep at night with crystals in your room. This is because the crystals are radiating their crystalline light into your energy field. In this case, just move the crystals outside the room, move one or two and see how it feels.

Recommended Crystals: Herkimer - Himalayan/New York origin, Brazilian Quartz, Angelite, Celestine, Apophyllite. *You can also include grounding crystals to assist in anchoring the crystalline light particularly for Brazilian Quartz – as it flows for you.

Crystals and Plants

I love placing beautiful plants amongst my crystals. It's a wonderful light connection to see in fruition. I like to rotate my plants that are flowering in pots and bring them inside amongst my crystals. A beautiful healthy plant amongst my favourite crystals is a lovely crystalline connection. You can notice the auric fields of the crystal and plants merging. A wonderful crystalline light convergence to see.

Candles, Plants & Crystals

The element of fire, the flame of a candle resonates a unique appeal and frequency to crystals. The crystalline frequency of the crystal will integrate with the auric field of the fire. It is a subtle yet beautiful light union. A lovely way to also see the Elemental beings of the flame and crystals integrate and play together in a higher dimensional field. Add some beautiful plants as well, enjoy this wonderful light union. A harmonic elemental dance of plant – crystal – fire devic beings. The combination of candles, plants and crystals is truly a wonderful alignment. Follow your instinct and light journey, as it will flow for you.

Crystals for Cleansing and grounding

Heart Chakra Cleanse and Empowerment, Protection

Morning exercise

To occur outside in the sun or inside in a comfortable space

*Choose crystals to hold, connect and expand

Close your eyes, take a moment to connect to your breath

Fill your heart with unconditional love - allow it to expand - visualise light expanding entering your heart - empowering your heart chakra (1-2 minutes).

Expand the light to cover your entire auric field.

Feel the power of you, acknowledge the strength of who you are.

Ask this light energy to shield you for your entire day, week, as it flows for you. Only allow high vibrational loving energies to interact with you.

This will act as a buffer to support your day and will greatly assist you in feeling centered and grounded, unconditional love and personal empowerment.

Everyone who interacts with you will feel a sense of peace and enlightenment.

A wonderful daily practice to assist your journey

Crystals for Grounding

Using crystals to ground and balance your light field, plays an important role in staying focussed and in tune with your mission.

A good way to check if you are grounded/or not grounded is to ask yourself, how AM I feeling? These physical and emotional symptoms could be related to a number of physical issues, including your diet, emotional relationships etc.

Some clues:

- Quickly losing energy
- A heightened sense of panic and emotions
- Flighty, emotions up and down and spontaneous actions
- Craving sugary foods

Being in these modes, can be very draining on the physical body. To sustain this mode, you could be craving unhealthy food to keep you in this heightened energy field. And this is very draining and tiring to the body. An easy way to fall into this pattern is not eating a good balanced diet, not having enough sleep, being emotionally unbalanced or dealing with extreme trauma.

If you continue in such a pattern, this can impact many areas of your life including your physical body and overall journey. Therefore, it's important to be conscious of your actions, for this will relate to how crystals can assist you.

Crystals for grounding: Haematite, Red Jasper, a local stone from your garden

Simply sit on the earth - anchor light from the ground

Hug a tree, drink filtered water for cleansing

Hold or wear crystals: hematite, red jasper, a stone from the garden.

Grounding light meditations; bask in the sun.

Creative Visualisation with Crystals

Energetically and physically, we can assist our life mission by using the crystalline frequency of crystals to visualise our goals, clear energy and raise our vibrational field to ensure we can manifest at a fast-productive pace.

Visualising your end goal and surrounding yourself will high vibrational frequencies, particularly crystal frequencies will really assist the unfolding of your dreams. For the manifestation of our dreams and desires is greatly assisted with high vibrational light frequencies.

You can still connect to crystal frequencies without crystals in your personal possession. Because our world is filled with crystalline frequencies connecting to these crystalline energy fields only requires imagination. You can also use stones in your garden if you feel the crystalline light connection, for grounding, anchoring light and manifestation. You can also use photos of crystals for your vision boards.

To learn about Crystal Grids and manifestation, go to the Crystal Grid section in this book to assist your light manifestation.

Cleansing your Crystals

I particularly enjoy two methods for Crystal cleansing, the sun and earth to cleanse and charge my crystals and Crystalline Light Visualisation.

The Cleansing Sun and Land

I love the morning vibrational frequencies of the sun; I rest my crystals on soft grass or the beautiful bare earth. It gives the crystals an opportunity to connect to the crystalline frequencies of the land, plants and local elementals, integrate and connect to Gaia. I choose a place that feels right, sheltered so the crystals can stay for a while – as it flows.

Visit the crystals and feel into their light field to determine if they are cleansed. They will feel and look brighter. It's ideal to choose a shaded location. A few hours will be adequate.

Thank the land, the special place and all beings that assisted cleansing the crystals.

Crystalline Light Visualisation

Simply hold the crystal in your hand, fill your auric field with light and visualise this light pouring and cleansing over your crystal. Simply feel into the crystal to know it is cleansed.

Understanding Entities & Attachment

As our world raises in higher light frequency, we learn about our connection to source and all beings in our world.

The more you evolve and awaken to your heart centre, you will naturally repel negative light beings. Simply because the advancement of your light field will be resilient and in an integrated alignment with your higher self. To reach this state of light attunement, for many it will involve light challenges to reach this stage of advancement.

Amongst all of this, always be aware of your intention to serve humanity and to be with one with the Universe. Work from the highest vibrational space of LOVE. For if you choose to work in the higher realms, you must be aware of each interaction. Ensure your space is cleansed and protected.

As you become more aware of your light field and your vibrational space, you will be able to vibrationally sense changes to the energy in a room, connect and understand how this energy feels. You may receive visions in your third eye, words and information associated with the energetic frequency. Other ways of connecting to beings is in the dream state. Depending on the type of dream will determine the kind of interactions with beings. And thus, from a dream, you can interpret the meaning of the dream.

Negative entities can come in many forms, for they enter your world and light field for a particular reason. As souls travel the lower dimensional planes, it is the aim of all beings to reach the white light to their collective soul family. Many are simply earth bound, in some cases they were abruptly moved from the physical body and are in a state of disarray and have yet to reach the light to the other side. For there are many scenarios from ancient times leading us to this now moment.

Physical and crystalline implants are also possible, resulting from other beings connecting with your light field. In many cases, you may have provided permission for these energetic, physical interactions. It is often not the case, and there is a process involved with removing such crystalline high-tech devices. Simply working with a Shamanic Healer/advanced Vibrational Light Healer can assist this process of removal and higher light expansion.

Cleanse your space, work in a space of love.
Be aware of your physical and non-physical interactions.
Be in Light.

Crystal Tools For Expansion and Healing

As you EXPAND

ALIGN to your LIGHT

ENHANCE your LIGHT SKILLS

BE the HEALER you SEEK

Spiral Dream Weaving

Gateway to the Higher Dimensions

Spiral Light Frequency

To assist in a deeper understanding of crystal grids and the use of a wand.

A pattern used by the Ancients

Marked on sacred sites, for it resonates a deep level of internal knowing

Do you feel the connection dear one?

Have you felt the inner calling of the spiral, but haven't been able to truly place the meaning for you?

We shall explain...

The spiral pattern is a GATEWAY to the Higher Dimensions

It acts as a WORMHOLE - allowing you to travel to the Higher Dimensions.

A skill widely used by those with the activated DNA, known as Shamans.

The transmutation of Gaia and all beings enables you to connect to the Spiral Energy combined with the activation of your DNA to transverse your planet and the Higher Dimensions.

As you start travelling with your light body, know your capabilities are greatly expanding as you are being turned ON - DNA activating & awakening.

Know this is your future to transverse the Universe and your planet.

Find the galactic freedom you SEEK.

To use your Multidimensional Wings of LIGHT

Spiral Technique

- Use your writing hand to draw large spirals in the air
- As you do this, connect to the energy of the spiral
- Feel into the air, the elementals
- Feel into the EXPANSION
- Allow your mind to wonder, expand
- We ask you to start visualising the spiral as a three-dimensional image. Like a crop circle – a one dimensional - multidimensional image. Expand your visual creativity and perception of the spiral you create.

Allow it to flow – Expand your Light Field

See the great expansion before you, as you connect more deeply to crystals. You will naturally feel a great sense of your light body awareness and a greater perception of who you truly are, the Multidimensional, magical aspect of you.

The Crystal Grid

Geometric patterns throughout our planet relate to the complex intelligence of life. The ancient history of creation holds the key to higher dimensional magic in our dimension. Combining crystals into patterns, also relates to natural patterns we observe in history that were used by the Ancients.

Known as a crystal grid, integrating the crystalline intelligence of each crystal in unison with a chosen pattern. For you are creating a crystalline harmonic light frequency, a light creation. Together, the unique combination of crystals energetically forms a light unison to assist you. Crystalline grids can be created in ancient geometric shapes and circular patterns, connecting to spiral energy and the free-flowing construct of Gaia.

Crystal Grids were used in many ancient civilisations and indigenous groups as part of ceremony to reach a higher state of consciousness. They were part of creating a sacred space to connect with the ancestors and the higher dimensions. Beautiful stones and boulders in your natural landscape can simply be part of your grid, for they hold the crystalline resonance of your land.

Crystals are integrated throughout the crystalline grid of Gaia and assist in the transmutation of energy moving through her construct. I see the crystalline grid of Gaia like a crystalline structure of energetic lines that are interconnected above and below the earth, and it extends outside the circumference of Gaia. As the crystals are located throughout Gaia to assist in the integration of universal light codes showering our planet. The crystals harmonise and clear historic energetic frequencies and collectively are part of the living breathing system of Gaia.

Plants and Crystal Grids

Including plants in your crystal grid is a lovely way of connecting to the local elementals, the plant spirits and the Plant Kingdom. Always invite the plant to be part of your grid. Ask for an energetic sign, a vibrational message, a free-flowing good energy feeling. The Plant Kingdom has an integral role to play, for they resonate their own matrix of light encoded frequencies. As we align to certain plants, as they are part of our living landscape, it is a lovely way to connect to the crystalline frequency of plants.

We are the wisdom keepers of divine light, we hold the codes of transformation and creation

Stonehenge could be classified as a Crystal Grid, composed of pillars of ancient rock that occur in a systematic pattern, used by the ancients for healing, initiations, a portal for multidimensional travel and an astronomical device. Natural outcrops and emerging boulders throughout the earth all have their role to play in maintaining and enhancing the crystalline structure of Gaia. For example, Uluru occurs in central Australia and has a pivotal role in anchoring light codes and the crystalline frequencies that is transmuted in that region and throughout the world. See each rock or boulder as important energy outlets and transmuters of high dimensional frequencies.

Setting the intention and the reason for creating a crystal grid will assist in the manifestation of your desires and outcomes. Your guides/team will assist as you choose your crystals and place your crystals in a particular shape or circular pattern.

Structure of a Crystal Grid ∞ Energy Flow

The energetic flow of your grid will be determined by the crystals you choose and the location of each crystal. To place a crystal in the centre of your grid will act as an energetic conduit, a central energy transmitter connecting all other crystals. The central crystal can influence the overall frequency of your grid, for I believe the central grid, roots and connects all crystals within your grid. Depending on the shape of your grid, you may not need a central or main crystal, so allow it to flow and see what feels right for you. Follow your intuition and go with the flow. Allow your intuition to guide your pattern, it's a beautiful way of expressing your energetic flow, following your internal guidance.

Including other objects, such as copper to enhance the crystalline frequency, a photo, piece of jewellery, a shell or piece of wood are other ideas. Follow your flow and intuition.

Grid Design

Using a geometric grid is a common way to create a crystal grid, as you lay your crystals on a geometric pattern. I could write about the complexities of each design and the reason for potentially choosing a geometric pattern. However, I'm more inclined to ask you to follow your intuition for creating a grid design. Crystal grids are part of your birth right, a connection to Gaia, to all living beings that reside on planet earth. It is a crystalline pattern within you, so feel into the design that you choose, experiment.

Preparing your space

- Prior to starting your crystal grid cleanse your space and home
- Cleanse your auric field
- Cleanse all of your crystals

Creating a grid

The power of intention and manifestation is a really important part of creating your grid. It is worth spending a week or two really thinking about the purpose and intent of your grid. As you focus on your reason, you may find the actual intention could change as you fine tune the reasons for creating a grid.

- In the first week write the reasons for creating a crystal grid.
- Some ideas: enhance a specific goal, manifest a particular object, improve relationships, clear and protect your home.
- In the second week, start drawing ideas connected to the shape of the grid. Think about the crystals that will assist you with emotional support leading up to your goal.

Choosing Crystals

As you become familiar with your specific goal and intention. Prior to choosing the crystals, brainstorm the associated feelings to reach your goal and the feelings achieved once you reach the goal. For example, if you wish to create a grid for psychic protection, you would list the feelings associated with being attacked through to being protected, happy and free flowing. From this point forward, think of the crystals that would assist you from protection to feeling loved, secure and grounded.

- Choose crystals that you love to work with, that you have an infinite relationship with, that are part of your Crystal Family. I love buying new crystals to use in my crystal grids. For what you purchase, or what you intend to purchase could be different to what you bring home. There is no rule to what you use, I just go with the flow and see what will evolve. If I am feeling I need to include more love frequencies, I will include Rose Quartz which is a big part of my personal collection.
- Write a list of the emotions and emotional outcomes you wish to achieve, so you can become familiar with the kind of crystals you need.
- Write a list of the crystals you wish to use. Or another way of doing this is to be with your crystals and connect to them. Intentionally feel which crystals you would like to work with and vice versa.
- Place your chosen crystals together to start growing your crystal grid collection.

Laying your grid

- As you lead up to the day, prepare yourself, your space and auric field. Cleanse yourself, your home and crystal grid space.
- Choose a place that feels right for you. It could be in a sacred healing space or your garden. Many have a sacred altar in their home, this could be a good place to keep your grid. I tend to choose a space where others can't touch or impact the flow of the grid.
- Put all of your crystals together, close your eyes and visualise the pattern you should use for your grid. Have a pen and paper with you to draw the designs that come through. Choose your design. Alternatively, you can just move your crystals and create a shape that suits. As it flows for you.

Activating your grid

- Place in your hand a piece of quartz, Selenite or a particular crystal that powerfully resonates for you. A wand is also another tool to use.
- As the crystal grid is in place, sit with your crystal grid.
- Observe the colours of the crystals, the alignment of the crystals.
- Close your eyes and see the energetic patterns of the crystal grid in your consciousness.
- Connect to your heart and feel the glow and expansion of your heart space. Align to the crystal grid and the intention. Open your heart space to your Soul Team and Angelic Light family. Ask for their assistance with the expansion of your crystalline grid frequencies. Call on the Crystal Devic beings to assist you in connecting to the Crystalline Crystal frequency of all crystals together in your grid.
- Open your eyes and feel the connection in this moment. The energy of the grid and your intention for the grid.
- With your writing hand, in a circular motion. I typically go clockwise, move your hand with the intention of activating the crystal grid. Feel this as a synchronistic connection, for the crystalline light of the crystals in the grid are uniting and moving in a harmonic convergence of light. Continue your hand motion until you feel the crystals are aligned in a harmonic frequency.
- Sit with your crystal grid and thank your soul team and all light beings who assisted.

The Crystal Wand

A crystal wand is a magical and beautiful way of initiating yourself to a higher expansive space and connection to your divine self. Owning a wand is a very special gift to yourself, for it activates a very special aspect of you. For it awakens memories of past lives, when magic was the norm within your daily way of being. When a wand or other light tools were of regular use, part of your interdimensional reality. We are intuitively connecting to these aspects of ourselves and feeling the internal powerful calling.

Choosing your wand is a very personal choice. You can start with any sort of wand, or even choose to make your own. I tend to own a few wands as they are an integral part of my healing work. As I feel the calling…. You can start with choosing a special stick found in a park or forest and attaching crystals or anything that resonates. Or simply the stick could be all you need…. For the tools of our natural world are very powerful and resonate their own crystalline light frequency to assist all beings.

Wands are a special tool for the healer, a direct tool to higher crystalline energy. The motions used with your hands also radiates the energy directed out of the tip of your wand. Like a beautiful symphony of light, a wand is an extension of your energetic healing light.

I particularly like to have a quartz point at the end of my wand, although other crystals work perfectly well and have their place in light healing. Following your light flow and intuition to choose your crystal wand.

Purchasing a wand

Prior to the purchase, I ask you to integrate all that you know about yourself and your crystal journey. Spend a moment thinking about your reason for purchasing a wand or creating a wand. What is your intention? What is your reason for requiring this tool? Perhaps spend some time writing in your journal. This will enable you to learn more about yourself and connect more deeply to your inner wisdom and guidance. Your needs will emerge as to why you feel inclined to purchase a wand. In many cases, it could be related to a past life when you used a wand. For you are calling forth your healing talents from other lives. You may connect to the frequency of an ancient wand used in many lifetimes. Think about the crystals you would like, the kind of wand you desire and need. Simply allow it to flow...

Initiating and cleansing your wand

Like all crystals you bring into your home, into your personal space, I feel it's important to welcome and integrate your wand and all healing tools into your home. I like to place my wand and crystals in my garden first. I have a special place for crystals to lay in my garden, connect to the earth and the local elementals. It's a place that is away from direct sun and will enable cleansing and crystalline alignment. Once I feel my wand is integrated, cleared and aligned, I send a crystalline invitation to welcome the wand in my home and healing space.

Using your wand

I ask you to follow your intuition, follow your innate connection and the energetic construct of your wand. As our DNA is more activated, our magical skills are awakening. For we feel the internal light calling, as we follow our intuition to reach our desired goals on our Mission of Light.

My advice is to connect to the Spiral energy, awaken to your intuition and do what feels right for you. Be the wayshower of your future and destiny. For your internal light is shining brighter as our multidimensional selves unite.

The Pendulum

I've found pendulums to be a useful tool to learn about the crystalline health of the chakras and the auric field. Place a pendulum above the chakra. If the pendulum spins in a certain direction or moves from side to side, it will provide insights about the energetic field and direction of the energy system of the chakra. Use your intuition to seek understanding about chakra health.

I would recommend using a beautiful hand carved wooden pendulum for investigative energy healing work, so the crystalline light field is not influenced by the vibrational frequency of a crystal. With saying this, know it is purely based on your personal choice and intuition. For the light journey is forever expanding work directly with your team for guidance.

As you have reached the final page of light wisdom. The final following pages provide important information for you dear one.

Crystalline Light Wisdom

Know your Crystal Light Journey is a special opportunity for Light Advancement. As our world is Awakening, as we join in Global Unity.

Know the path is unique for each of us, as we walk the higher light path of true awakening. There is no right or wrong path, leading you to a space of greater light expansion. It is simply the task of seeing your internal truth, finding your light mission trajectory to shine your light for humanity.

Sending much love for your journey. Know my heart is filled with joy for those who read this passage. For like you, I am an intrepid awakener to light. As we all journey forth to assist Humanity and Mother Gaia.

Harmony, Unity, Love

Thank you for
Shining Your Light

For opening your HEART to Peace

For following your Path and Mission

For Seeking Truth

As we Awaken

To the greater knowing of who WE ARE

I ask you to acknowledge the great work you have achieved dear one

To continue expanding your Heart - Mind connection.

To Live in a HEART space of Purity and Light.

As we join in Global UNITY and connect to Mother Gaia

LOVE and INFINITE

BLESSINGS

Karen Lithika

Crystal Light Guardian©
WORKSHOP

Learn multidimensional crystalline light tools

Develop your crystalline intuition

Crystal communication, attunement

Learn new crystalline light information

New techniques for crystal healing

Come along on a Crystal Light Journey

visit KarenLitika.com

For the latest workshop dates

Karen Lithika

Karen Lithika is a Crystal Vibrational Healer, Botanist, with a PhD in Australian lilies.

Karen's innate connection to her soul family enables her to channel a myriad of light beings. She assists clients worldwide with personal light healing, using a myriad of light tools including Multidimensional Light Body Crystal Healing.

Karen also offers group Higher Realm journeys and numerous workshops to develop your personal Light Ascension gifts and Crystal Light Expansion.

To follow updates, visit Karen on social media, join the mailing list on her website, visit KarenLithika.com.

Together we align in Higher Light, in a space of Love and Unity on beautiful Mother Gaia.

With Love and Blessings for your Ascension Journey.

Global Light Blessings

Karen Lithika

Crystal Guardians of Gaia and New Earth

Multidimensional Crystal and Planetary Wisdom

Discover invaluable information about the history and birthing of crystals, their purpose in assisting Humanity and Gaia's Ascension.

- Learn about the Crystal Akashic Records and Crystals in the higher dimensions
- Discover how to open your consciousness to crystal communication
- Find new powerful ways to work with Crystals as a Crystal Light Guardian
- Learn new techniques to expand your healing modalities

Many millennia ago, crystals were a fundamental part of society. They were used in all aspects of energy healing, portal travelling and living a higher vibrational existence. Today, crystals are now assisting Humanity to remember their ancestral origins and innate crystalline connection to energy.

As our light bodies rise to a higher vibrational frequency, we become more aware of the crystalline frequency of crystals, their messages and integrations within our light bodies.

Embrace the Crystalline Light Journey before you, as we journey to Light.

Notes

Notes

Notes

Notes

Notes

Notes

Printed in Great Britain
by Amazon